The Hospital Handbook

REVISED EDITION

THE
HOSPITAL
HANDBOOK

A Practical Guide to Hospital Visitation

Lawrence D. Reimer
James T. Wagner

Foreword
Wayne E. Oates

MOREHOUSE PUBLISHING
Harrisburg, PA

We acknowledge with gratitude the following permissions:

- from *The New English Bible.* © The Delegates of the Oxford University Press and The Syndics of the Cambridge University Press, 1961, 1970.

- from the *Good News Bible* copyright © American Bible Society, 1976.

- from *Psalms/Now* ©1973 by Concordia Publishing House.

- from the *Revised Standard Version of the Bible,* copyrighted 1946, 1952 © 1971, 1973, the Division of Education and Ministry of the National Council of Churches of Christ. (Some RSV passages have been slightly altered, with the Division's consent, to reflect inclusive language.)

Morehouse Publishing
P.O. Box 1321
Harrisburg, PA 17105

Library of Congress Cataloging-in-Publication Data

Reimer, Lawrence D.
  The hospital handbook.

  Includes bibliographies.

  1. Church work with the sick—Handbooks, manuals, etc. 2. Pastoral medicine—Handbooks, manuals, etc.
I. Wagner, James T.   II. Title.
BV4335.R43   1988   259'.4   88-1790

ISBN 0-8192-1470-1 (pbk.)

Printed in the United States of America

Third Printing, 1994

Dedication

to Mary Anne
and
Scott Wagner

Sandy,
Matthew
and
Christopher Reimer

CONTENTS

Charles A. Williams, M.D.
Department of Pediatrics
University of Florida

Foreword

Wayne E. Oates, Ph.D

For a long time this book by Pastor Lawrence Reimer and Chaplain James Wagner has been needed. The unique focus of the book is embodied in the personal dialogue between these two under-shepherds of Jesus Christ, one a chaplain "inside" the hospital staff and the other a pastor visiting in the hospital from the "outside."

I first sensed the need of such a book early in my ministry. I was a student chaplain in a program of clinical pastoral education. I visited and cared for a certain patient and her family. A year and a half later I became the pastor of the church of which she and her family were members. She had become ill again and was admitted to the same hospital. I was asked to visit her then as her pastor, from outside the hospital. The very atmosphere and content of the relationship and conversation was dramatically different! I concluded that one reason for this was that I related to her on a temporary—or "one-layer" basis, to use Wagner's and Reimer's term—when I was a student chaplain. I related to her on a many-layered basis when I was her pastor. Both relationships had their strengths, but both had their limitations. They needed each other. Likewise, I was not a part of the hospital staff as her pastor. She associated me with another place, her church, not the hospital. "Hospital" meant to her, "sick"; "Church" to her meant "well enough to go to church!" I am happy indeed to discover this book that brings these two perspectives into dialogue with each other in the persons of these authors.

It was not until I had been privileged to read this book that I found a serious discussion of what a pastor experiences when he or she visits in a hospital "from the outside" and how he or she can inform, shape, and enrich these experiences to the greatest benefit to the patient.

The training of a pastor is remarkably deficient in dealing with what it is like and what is needed to visit the hospital from the outside, as a parish pastor routinely does. Usually in seminary-related and other programs of clinical pastoral education, the student works from "within" the hospital staff. He or she moves along with well established pathways of communication with staff, patients, and families that have been built by the faithfulness and credibility of the chaplain-supervisor. More than he or she is aware, the student is in a protected situation. In gaining entrance to staff conferences, nursing report times at changes of shifts, and even being allowed to visit certain patients, the clinical pastoral education student has a way opened by reason of the chaplain supervisor's longer term relationship. No such luxury is available to the pastor of a church from the outside, ordinarily, and especially is this true of a pastor newly arrived in a parish situation.

Chaplain Wagner and Pastor Reimer have spoken to this need of the parish pastor to find his or her way systematically into the sphere of relationships in a hospital staff, among attending physicians, families, and patients in the modern hospital. They have the courage to say things that are obvious to a person who works full time in the hospital but are as unintelligible as a foreign language or custom to many pastors. Much of what is communicated within a hospital is in code words and terms and in nonverbally understood rituals that cause many pastors to feel that they are in a "foreign territory." This book by Reimer and Wagner translates this "hospitalese" into pastorally meaningful concepts that both pastor and lay visitor can understand, appreciate, and appropriate.

Similarly, the hospital has an elaborate set of medical rituals of diagnosis, treatment plans, ways of prolonging life, responses to emergency threats to life, and caring for the desperately ill and dying patient. The authors of this manual make you comfortably aware of what these rituals are and what they mean. They give you concrete suggestions as to how, where, and when you can bring the rituals of your pastoral presence, your prayers, your reading of the healing grace of the Scriptures, and your infusion of the life of the church community into the support system of the patient. They emphasize the blend of your rituals or ways of doing things with those of the hospital community. The secret to the blending process is in your getting to know the staff, the attending physician, and the very personality of the corporate lives of the different kinds of hospitals in which you visit.

One thing these authors consistently express needs understanding here: they themselves very apparently *like* being ministers. They know that their identity as ministers is to them a unique gift related to the patient. for example, the pastor has appropriate access to any patient that needs him or her. The pastor is welcome in all areas of the hospital and not restricted to a special area or kind of patient. The pastor, most of all, is the one skilled in the use of words, in the patient listening to and speaking with a sick person. I summary, the pastoral heart of these authors beats regularly, in rhythm and with rubby vigor. They are forthright in their explicit directions concerning the ministry of prayer and the Word of the Scriptures. In this sense they bring into contemporary utterance the earlier wisdom of Cabot and Dicks in their classic book, *The Art of Ministering to the Sick.*

The authors of *The Hospital Handbook* have demonstrated that the hospital is a *community.* Your own sense of what a community is will be informed richly as to the nature and composition, stresses and strains of a community like a hospital. Furthermore, they give guidance as to how the pastor can multiply his or her effectiveness when he or she becomes personally and not just anonymously related to the members of this hospital community. Many references are made to physicians, nurses, and others who are members of *both* the hospital community *and* the church community of which one may be the pastor. In the last chapter they move the two communities into even closer relationship with each other. They give specific guidance for selecting, motivating, and educating lay persons in the church also to participate effectively in the care of the sick. Thus both pastor and chaplain become facilitators of the expression of the gifts of lay persons in their ministry to the sick. Moreover, they become catalysts of community at both places— the hospital and the church. Underneath these strategies of Reimer and Wagner is and implicit if not explicit appreciation of a systems approach to both hospital and church, both patient and family , both medicine and ministry.

A point of unusual concern in this book is its emphasis upon the pastoral care of the sick child and his or her family. One of the most profound passages in the book for me is as follows:

> All gifts and skills of the ministry come to focus in the experience of a child seriously ill. Perhaps no other life event renders persons so vulnerable. Deep within us there is a primitive if not profound notion that everyone should have a past. Any threats to a child's accruing a past become symbols of how unfair life can be and how in-

> justice is woven throughout the fabric of creation. Parents
> and other adults experience threats to the child as a feel-
> ing of having lost their future, their immortality. Offer-
> ing faith in God must be done in the face of these realities,
> not as a means to remove them. Having an adult faith
> means affirming life despite the world being harsh at
> times. Creation may be "good," but it is not perfect. In
> the child's illness there is a great challenge for pastor, pa-
> tient, family, and the entire caring community to
> undergird one another with faith, hope, and love. In time,
> hope and faith will return. Love, however, must never
> be absent.(p.65)

This poignant expression is especially true of the sick child but is
to some extent true of any serious illness of anyone. The theological
perception of the persistence of love in the face of the mystery of
human suffering that eclipses for a time hope and faith is not just
a jewel to be admired. It is a working principle for the pastor as he
or she travels between life and death with fellow mortals, as Richard
Baxter said, "as a dying person speaking to dying persons."

Reimer and Wagner, in this passage and in this book,
present the hospital as a powerful arena for genuine spiritual enquiry
in the face of the inscrutable mysteries of human suffering. It is an
honor for me to be permitted to present their work to you as a reader.

Wayne E. Oates, Ph.D.
Professor of Psychiatry and
Behavioral Sciences
School of Medicine,
University of Louisville
Louisville, Kentucky 40292
July 14, 1984

Acknowledgments

Our first acknowledgment is to each other as co-authors. Reimer is listed before Wagner in the title page out of deference to alphabetical order. We are friends and professional colleagues who have remained so throughout the writing of this book. This is a fully collaborative effort divided as evenly as anything could be divided. Secondly, we thank Charles A. Williams, M.D., who supplied the glossary of medical terms. We deeply appreciate his gift of making the obscure understandable to those of us who must cope with unfamiliar terms in the hospital environment.

We are also grateful to other clergy who have offered the benefits of their experiences in hospital visiting. They represent a broad range of denominations, geographical settings, and ministerial styles. Their stories and insights appear throughout the book. Therefore we thank A. Russell Ayre, Richard Bailar, Donald Bain, Robert Besalski, Richard Dietrich, Sue Gallagher, Rabbi Allan Lehmann, Donald Miller, Richard Sebastian, William Tuck, and John Rutland-Wallis. We thank the following mental health professionals from community and university settings who gave us useful perspectives on community resources and psychiatric hospitalization: Dr. James Archer, Dr. Mary Anna Hovey, and Dr. Douglas Starr. We appreciate the medical advice on technical questions supplied by Robert McCollough, M.D., and David Paulus, M.D.

Wayne Oates read this manuscript and immediately found those places we needed to fill gaps, make the vague specific, and add data. Barbara Beynon did much of the typing, and Ann Terrell managed the difficult task of final typing for two different authors. Stephen Wilburn of Morehouse Barlow had a contagious enthusiasm for this book which gave us just the encouragement we needed. We thank them all.

Finally, we wish to express our deep gratitude to the many patients and parishioners who have enriched this book by sharing themselves with us.

Acknowledgments are appropriate for contributions made to the revision. At Shands Hospital and the University of Florida's College of Medicine, Bill Treloar, Director of Case Mix Management, Loretta Fauerbach, Director of Infection Control, and Ray Moseley, Ph.D., Director of the Medical Humanities Program, made thoughtful and informed suggestions. Russell Clifton, Ph.D., of HCA Grant Center Hospital, and Tom Erney, Ph.D. of the Quest National Center, both reviewed information on adolescence and psychiatric hospitalization. Carolyn O'Boyle typed the revised portion of the manuscript.

Introduction

As Director of Pastoral Care at a major health care referral center, I continue to spend a great deal of time "keeping up" with what is happening in my own hospital. After fourteen years I keep having this fantasy that people will start coming to me to learn what is going on. It never happens. Somehow it goes with my role that I am the one who must initiate and maintain the working relationships.

For parish ministers, the difficulties of hospital visitation and ministry to the physically ill are certainly compounded by the fact that they are "outsiders" to the hospital staff. Unless a minister took clinical pastoral education courses in seminary, it is not likely that s/he had formal training in how to do hospital visitation. Consequently I am impressed that while ministers value pastoral care during the crisis of illness, many find hospital visiting frustrating.

And that is understandable. Physicians, nurses and other staff may appear somewhat unconcerned, if not abrupt with information and/or directions. Even when the pastor has traveled some distance, as is often the case at our hospital, the patient may be in x-ray, having a test run, or be inaccessible for any number of reasons. Even parking is sometimes difficult. All of this is frustrating for the clergyperson, if not intimidating, and adds additional stress to an already busy schedule.

The Hospital Handbook is an effort to provide the divinity student, the beginning pastor, and perhaps the experienced minister seeking a resource for lay visitors with practical guides to hospital ministry. Included are sections which discuss hospital organization, how to gain access to the system, and knowing what behaviors lead to cooperation with staff.

James T. Wagner, Ph.D.

In my first position as a parish minister, it suddenly dawned on me that I did not know where to begin in hospital visitation. I had attended a thoroughly respectable divinity school. I had taken the suggested courses. I knew the finer points of pastoral counseling, medical ethics, and the existential realities of suffering, but I did not know how to find a patient's room. I did not know aneurism from angina.

Fortunately, I began my ministery as an Associate Pastor, and the Senior Pastor was very understanding in showing me around the hospital, introducing me to key personnel, and giving me a good outline of the do's and don't's of hospital visiting. The key to that first learning experience was finding the right information at the right time. I had to learn, and Russ Ayre, the Senior Pastor, gave me clear, practical information.

That was fifteen years ago. The teachable moments have continued. There was the first encounter with a sick child, the dying patient, the need to consult with a physician, the time it was necessary to help a patient get a second medical opinion. There was the move to the community with the university teaching hospital, and the continued need to understand new medical terms. Sometimes the information was easy to get in order to deal with these hospital situations. Sometimes it was not. I wanted a *Hospital Handbook* to provide practical information for those critical times in pastoral care.

Jim Wagner is the insider at the hospital, the director of pastoral care who is an expert on keeping people like me informed on what is going on in the hospital and how to relate to these developments. I am the outsider, the parish minister who is an expert on reminding the insiders that we need simple, practical assistance in keeping up with our role in patient care.

Lawrence D. Reimer

INTRODUCTION TO THE REVISED EDITION:

We are grateful for the opportunity to do a revised edition. In the four years since the *Handbook* was published, we have maintained a careful file of suggestions from users and reviewers, as well as new material which we believed would strengthen the book. The growing number of readers deserves the best we can offer and Morehouse-Barlow agreed.

One dimension of the revision is to update some of the rapid changes occurring in the health care field. Most of these are reflected in Chapter One, sometimes accomplished by changing a verb from future to present or past tense. The issue identified at the end of this chapter, making health care available to all persons, remains a central focus of debate in America.

New material is to be found in several places. Chapter Four has been expanded with additional prayers, scripture references, and an order for the administration of the sacramemt of Holy Communion in a hospital setting. Chapter Five is considerably lengthened by sections which focus on the adolescent as well as the AIDS patient. Admissions of adolescents to specialized centers for the treatment of substance abuse and psychiatric problems are increasing. Ministry to adolescents in these special facilities as well as general hospitals involves unique issues addressed here. As hospital admissions for AIDS patients increases, ministry to these patients and families is clearly an important new pastoral concern. We invite readers to contribute their perspectives on the usefulness of this material. Charles Williams, M.D., has expanded the Glossary and polished all of the definitions.

A new chapter focuses the subject of Medical Ethics. The reader will find a helpful introduction to most of the situations relevant to hospital ministry. Familiarity should enhance the pastor's usefulness. As is true with the other chapters, readings in the form of an annotated bibliography are found at the end.

The *Handbook* is an effort to add new construction to the bridge connecting the pastor and the hospital. We hope the result will be an easier path for the minister in delivering pastoral care to parishioners. If the book proves useful and fulfills its limited goals, the authors will feel gratified. We made the decision long ago that the effort was worth it, because we believe strongly in the value of spiritual care during illness and its place in the delivery of wholistic health care.

We also hope this book encourages further cooperation between chaplains and pastors. Either of our names could appear first in authorship as the contributions of each have been similar. A small section of this book addresses the appropriate need and probable benefit of more frequent collaboration, particularly in critical life events such as illness.

No single book is adequate, however, to prepare a minister for the specific concerns which might be experienced. This book is directed to those situations most commonly encountered. Even then, it provides a general guide. For more specific information the reader is directed to the annotated bibliography at the end of each chapter as well as the glossary at the end of the book.

Today's Hospital
It's Not Like Where You Were Born

1

A Revolution
You Ought
to Know About
Hospitals are experiencing radical changes, some occurring even as you read this book. This revolution is of interest to pastors, lay-persons, and the Church for several reasons. A significant portion of your ministry is carried out in relationship to illness events. Understanding the nature and structure of hospitals can aid you toward working effectively within that system. Second, you and your parishioners utilize health care facilities as patients and being aware will assist you toward becoming an informed consumer. Third, it may be that some of these changes call for the Church to become more active, at least educationally, in the health care endeavor.

At the heart of this revolution are two central questions. Is health care a right to be afforded to all persons or is it available to the privileged only? Privileged usually means that you and/or a third party (insurance) will pay the bills. The second question is: Who is going to pay for the services? In our society the prevailing political answer[1] to the first question is that

---

1. In April 1983, the President's Commission for the Study of Ethical Problems in Medicine and Biomedical and Behavioral Research published a controversial report entitled *Securing Access to Health Care* (U.S. Government Printing Office, s/n 040-000-00472-9) which said, in part, that "society has the responsibility ethically to provide every person with an adequate level of health care without excessive burden to anyone." The Commission did not say that everybody in society who

Americans should have unlimited access to the best available health services. In order to provide the service, however, health care costs currently consume 10.7% of the gross national product.

This wasn't such a problem as long as the family doctor got in his car and drove to your home when you were ill. S/he usually had everything required for treatment in a black bag, predictably a tongue depressant, a stethoscope to listen to heart and lungs, a light to look in the ears or eyes, and, finally, a penicillin shot. As technology developed, however, a clustering of services resulted. Physicians preferred to locate offices near hospitals, which became the centers for the treatment of illness. You now go to the physician's office for care and, if necessary, can be admitted to the nearby hospital, reducing travel time between office and hospital for the doctor.

It has been theorized that when physician house calls became uncommon,[2] the sanctity of the physician-relationship changed forever. In its place emerged a less personal, more technological approach which can save lives, but also can prolong life unnecessarily, always at a high cost. There is the resulting need continuously to refurbish and replace outdated hospital facilities and to have the latest piece of new technology. Physicians' salaries have skyrocketed, yet patient-physician relationships have grown even more impersonal, which contributes to a litigious climate. This climate results in higher malpractice insurance premiums, the ordering of more tests for defensive purposes, and higher costs for the patient. The spiral of increasing costs has been staggering. Controlling these costs and preserving the availability of health care has become a national concern.

Private For Profit, Not-For-Profit   To address these problems, changes are occurring both within and without the hospital. Externally, a recent change (October 1983) was made by the Federal Government. Previously, Medicare reimbursed hospitals for actual costs based on services delivered when

---

could not afford it privately or cannot get it through other resources, is entitled to all the care that the person wants or all the care that may be beneficial. This is a position quite different from that which is politically expressed but may, in fact, more accurately describe what occurs in our society.

2.   Meg Cox, "This Doctor Says: Take Two Aspirins and I'll Call on You in the Morning," The Wall Street Journal, January 5, 1984, p. 25. The best available figures indicate that physician house calls dropped to 17 million in 1975 from 60 million in 1960.

a patient covered by the program was admitted for treatment. Now a complicated reimbursement program has been implemented over a multi-year span which is based on diagnostic categories of illnesses and is referred to as prospective payment.[3] What this means is that hospitals will know in advance what Medicare will pay for the treatment of a particular illness. If the hospital can provide service for less than Medicare will pay, it can keep the balance as profit. Should their costs exceed the amount reimbursed, however, the hospital experiences a loss. As was predicted, most insurers have followed a similar fixed reimbursement formula.

In response, as you can imagine, hospitals and medical staffs are having to re-learn much of their way of providing health care. Some of these changes are positive and others will create further problems in the future. For example, tests which are not critical for the patient's treatment will no longer be performed. This should lower costs for everyone. On the other hand, hospitals have at times provided very humane services which will also necessarily be discontinued. The patient ready for discharge but who has nowhere to go will not be cared for in the hospital until other arrangements can be effected. Again, some illnesses may become viewed as desirable admissions due to their proven profitability for the hospital. Others, however, which become known as marginal, may be avoided. Today, many of the "for profit" hospitals will not provide pediatrics, obstetrics-gynecology, psychiatric or emergency services as they are known to be cost-inefficient.

Other outside agencies exist which seek to guide the development of hospitals. Federal and State cost containment and review groups must approve price increases, allocation of beds, and new construction in an effort to avoid an abundance of resources which would lead to ever increasing costs. By the mid-1970s these outside agencies made hospitals one of the most highly regulated enterprises in the United States.[4] The response of the health care industry has left the neighborhood hospital where you were born ill-prepared to cope with the new structures which are emerging. The hospital will soon be only a part of the effort to treat and /or prevent illness. The emerging structure is that of the Health Care System, a corporate or holding company model.

---

3. Social Security Amendments of 1983, Pub. L No. 98–21, 601–07, 97 Stat. 65, 149–72 (1983). (Prospective payment for Medicare inpatient hospital services based on DRGs.)
4. F.H. Kerr, "Considering a New Structure: The Health Services Holding Company," *Law, Medicine and Health Care*, Vol. 11, No. 5, October 1983, p. 214.

The function of the "system" is to capture a significant portion of the health care market in its geographic region. It is a business approach with key notions being "cost containment" and "revenue production" without compromise in quality of care. To achieve these goals, the system must structure itself to accomplish two things. First, it must market health care, including preventive and rehabilitative functions. This means offering a diversification of services, some of which were originally provided by the hospital. This is a reversal in the earlier trend to center activities in the hospital. Second, each division in the system becomes a referral source to the hospital, in order to maximize occupancy rates, and, in turn, the hospital refers back to other parts of the system for its specializations.

The changes in the hospital structure relate both to its role in the system and the severe regulations described earlier which govern its functioning. Rate reviews, price structuring, and prospective payment, for example, do not currently apply to outpatient services but only to inpatient hospitalization. Consequently, the system will seek to "unbundle" hospital services and separate out any function which can be independently organized. Some of the more common services which have been unbundled are surgery procedures which can be done on an outpatient basis. "Surgi-Centers" are the result. Emergency clinics are another illustration. Not only can the system charge more for services provided by these facilities, but, should the patient require more serious attention, s/he can be referred to the system's hospital. If the patient has experienced a stroke and is treated at the hospital, upon discharge the patient can be referred to the system's "Wellness Center" or "rehabilitation program" for recuperative care.

Economic restraints on the hospital have resulted in the necessity to restructure health care delivery. Marketing this health care has fashioned a much broader, more wholistic approach. It is quite different from the single-minded acute care facility which has been the identity of most hospitals. In the system the hospital is only one dimension, although it remains the central one.

Obviously, other disadvantages await the neighborhood hospital which continues to try and stand alone. Larger systems will either link themselves in cooperative voluntary ventures or be owned/leased outright by corporate structures, as in the case of Hospital Corporation of America. By virtue of size, purchasing and personnel advantages abound. Supplies can be bought at such volume to assure discounts when compared to single unit purchases. It is hoped that these savings can be passed on to the patient. If this is true, then the patient will prefer to select admission to a hospital which is part of a larger system, and not the local, independent, neighborhood hospital. An idea which improves health care can be duplicated throughout similar facilities in a larger system. As well, the system may only have to employ one person with high-tech skills, sharing the costs, and make him available to all parts of the system. These are but a few examples of other advantages when systems are compared to your free-standing, neighborhood hospital.

The changes which this revolution represent are an industry's efforts to meet the need of providing health care services at a reasonable cost. These changes are in their early stages and their impact is not yet clearly known. They attempt to be more cost efficient for consumers while being businesslike in approach. Clearly, if the system fails in this country, the persons hurt most will be those who have the least ability to gain adequate care: the poor, the disabled, and those on fixed incomes.

Meaning For Ministry, Lay Persons, and the Church   Unlike the free-standing hospital of the past, which provided crisis intervention when illness or accident occurred, the system will market health care. Persons who wish to participate in maintaining or enhancing their state of health will find organizations such as Wellness Centers available. In this sense, the shape of health care will become more wholistic, which is a positive development. The dimensions of health which systems will find themselves least able to provide, however, have to do with life questions of meaning and purpose.

These are spiritual concerns which have as much to do with our health as good nutrition, proper exercise, and stress management. Although chaplains and social workers will continue to be employed by hospitals, the need for the Church's ministry during the crisis of illness will probably increase. This will be true because of several factors, all related to illness being a "teachable moment" that invites a re-examination of life values. First, the patient's experience of hospitalization will likely become more brief and intense. Inpatient days will be reduced. There will be less time in the hospital, both before and after the onset of illness or having surgery. Second, opportunities to review life experiences and reframe values and priorities will be minimized. Yet questions like "Why is this happening to me?" "What meaning does it have for my life?" "What have I learned?" remain important in the adjustment and recovery process.

What is being communicated here is not that pastoral ministry to ill persons is new or that pastors have neglected their parishioners. The message is that the need for the Church's ministry is heightened by the changes going on in hospitals. In his popular book *Megatrends*,[5] John Naisbitt talks about the growth of high technology creating a corresponding need for "high-touch." It is not the intent of hospitals to be less personal as they become more businesslike and as medicine relies increasingly on new technology. It will happen, nevertheless. The patient's need will grow for someone to enter his life who has no form for them to complete, no technology to be explained, no procedure to be done. The pastor is someone who can sit quietly, hear what the patient is feeling, respond with empathy, and relate it to a faith that enhances healing and wholeness.

This same need for "high-touch" exists for persons who work in hospitals. The new technology saves lives, but it can also prolong and unnecessarily complicate dying. It isn't simply that a respirator frustrates the natural occurrence of death. More critically, a machine that can breathe for you has almost become a part of the natural order. In the case of reversible causes, such as a drug overdose, the respirator breathes for you until life is safe and recovery under way. The emotional problems which lead to the overdose can then be sorted through. In other cases, the respirator provides needed time to evaluate and diagnose, or to give further treatment. But when it is believed, but not yet a certainty, that meaningful life is not possible, no uncomplicated decision-making process exists to discontinue life-sustaining treatment.[6] Hospital staff need the sustenance of their faith to adequately cope with the stress of being responsible for difficult decision-making.

Ministers and churches need also to be aware that, as health care systems and participating hospitals become more competitive, they also become more sensitive to public relations and community opinion. The Church can encourage support for chaplaincy as well as the pastoral care of individual ministers by communicating with the administrations or boards of the hospital. There are many services churches can provide to hospitals. For example, almost every hospital has an auxiliary for volunteers. A church which invites the director of that service to speak and

---

5. J. Naisbitt, *Megatrends*. New York: Warner Books, 1982, pp. 39–53.

6. "Deciding to Forego Life-Sustaining Treatment," President's Commission for the Study of Ethical Problems in Medicine and Biomedical and Behavioral Research, March 1983. (Suite 555, 2000 K Street, N.W., Washington, D.C. 20006.)

X

encourages participation breeds good will. Parishioners hospitalized can communicate their appreciation for a chaplain's visit or the accessibility to their pastor, even in an intensive care unit. Obviously, any church expressing these interests must represent needs and concerns common to every denomination and not attempt to manipulate personal advantages. At times, a responsible Ministerial Association can assume this role.

Just as pastors are gaining new understanding regarding the emergence of health care delivery systems, parishioners will benefit from a similar exploration. Perhaps the idea of establishing a Health Care Committee in your church would assist in educating members to these new structures. Other, equally important concerns need exploring also. For example, most major faith groups are increasingly relying upon lay persons to provide ministry during life crises. Although a chapter of this book discusses the topic of lay ministry in depth, a Health Cabinet can provide a portion of that education.

Moreover, there are several direct ways in which the Church's educational program can speak directly to the national issues of preserving availability of health care and cost containment. First, the Church can remind its membership of stewardship which relates to care of the body. The larger issue is that of preventive health care. It is hoped that research will soon emerge to provide cures for many types of cancer. Even if this happens, most of the dramatic breakthroughs which impacted so positively on health, like the discovery of germ theory, antibiotics, and polio vaccine are past history. Most authorities agree that the major breakthroughs lie in the realm of individuals adjusting their life style, specifically reducing caloric intake, eating better foods, exercising more, and learning to manage stress. The major killers, such as coronary artery disease, strokes, and hypertension, cannot be cured with a vaccine. The Church should take a more active role in spreading the "good news" which relates to an abundant, physically healthy life.

Second, containing costs of health care is not simply the responsibility of physicians and hospitals. The need is for all persons to become informed consumers. Out of a false sense of fidelity, for example, an individual might decide against seeking a second medical opinion. Checking into a hospital on a weekend, apart from an emergency, will usually not result in any meaningful treatment until a weekday, but it increases costs to the consumer. Being hospitalized for minor surgery because you are reluctant to investigate an out-patient alternative does not mean you will receive better care. It does guarantee higher bills. The patient-physician relationship previously characterized as paternalistic but now becoming more collaborative is probably a healthy one.

Yet none of these changes is easy, not for individuals nor for institutions such as the health care system. What motivates the changes is the necessity to preserve availability of health care at a cost that is affordable to all. That is the hope. The voice of the Church and ministry is a powerful one. Informed and aware, it can assist in shaping the structures and practices which develop. Historically, it can continue to be a meaningful part of a life experience that is common to all. Its ministry, in both professional and lay forms, must be prepared to increase input. The alternative is further fragmentation of life experience, particularly the search for meaning and purpose in the midst of life crises.

Bibliography

Cousins, N. *Anatomy of an Illness.* New York: W.W. Norton Co., Inc. 1979.
    The author recovers from a serious illness through following standard medical regimens in addition to his own prescriptions. This book is now a classic and highlights partnership between physician and patient.
Cousins, N. *The Healing Heart.* New York: W.W. Norton Co., Inc., 1984.
    Cousins offers personal reflections on ways he managed his recovery from a significant heart attack through monitoring his own anxiety and developing a partnership with medical staff.
Florell, J.L. "Wholistic Health and Pastoral Counseling." *Journal of Pastoral Care.* Vol. XXXIII, No. 2, June 1979, pp. 96–103.
    Presents an overview of approaches to wholistic health care in a variety of settings.
Goldsmith, J.C. *Can Hospitals Survive?* Homewood,Il.: Dow Jones-Irwin, 1981.
    The author puts forth a thoughtful and insightful discussion of the major changes occurring in the health care field. He describes the already intense competition among hospitals, which is resulting in restructuring of the entire system. Consumer choice as well as cost consciousness are guiding principles which will result in the closing of some facilities and the survival of others.
Tubesing, D.A. *Wholistic Health.* New York: Human Sciences Press, 1979.
    The author provides an excellent comparison and contrast between traditional models of providing health care and those which include a wholistic philosophy. As a single resource it provides an excellent discussion of the issues.
Westberg, R. "From Hospital Chaplaincy to Wholistic Health Center." *Journal of Pastoral Care.* Vol. XXXIII, No. s, June 1979, pp. 76–82.
    Reports on developing programs bringing patients into the diagnostic and healing process.

You're an Outsider: How Do You Get Inside? 2

I write this chapter as a parish minister who spent a year hunting for parking spaces at one hospital before I discovered there was a special permit for ministers. I have visited more empty rooms than I care to mention. I have served in communities where everyone who did not know what denomination they were listed themselves as a member of my denomination when they checked into the hospital. And I have served in other communities where no one had ever heard of my denomination, including the people at the hospital information desk. I have heard the stories of countless other pastors who have struggled with the logistics of hospital visitation.

People Who Can Help   When you arrive in a new community, establish a plan to get acquainted with the hospitals and physicians who care for your congregation. Such a plan should begin with the physicians who are members of your congregation. Ask your parishioners for other names of the community's respected doctors as well. Call these key medical people and ask for an opportunity to meet with them at their convenience. Breakfast, lunch, a cup of coffee after rounds at the hospital, are all possible times to introduce yourself. Let these physicians tell you about their community, the current issues at the local and regional hospitals, and the needs they see for visiting and pastoral care. Find out how to share information about patients when necessary. Ask for the names of other health professionals they feel you should meet. Use all these contacts as a time to get to know each other. Specific questions and critical concerns may arise later. These will be much easier to deal with if you have first established a firm base of personal trust.

Before your first hospital call, find someone who can give you an orientation to the hospital. In a large hospital this might be the chaplain. If there is no chaplain, there are social workers, administrators, and staff with a title such as hospital hostess who can give you a tour, explain that hospital's policies for clergy visits, and even help you find a place to park your car.

If you cannot find someone within the hospital to help, ask another pastor in the community. Along the way, make sure your guide introduces you to key hospital personnel. You will be spending a lot of time in the hospital. It is important for hospital staff to recognize you and for you to know whom to call when you have special concerns.

It is clear that many of the logistical elements of hospital visiting are determined by the size of the hospital, community, and church where you work. In Connecticut I was on the staff of a large church, in the largest denomination in the state, in a small town, in a small hospital. There was always someone to see in the hospital, so I just went regularly. I didn't always know everyone I saw, but the hospital personnel got to know me quickly. It was easy to find patients from my church in the visitor's directory. When I moved to Florida, I found myself in a community with four large hospitals, in a small church, of a denomination most people in the South had never heard of. My hospital visiting in Florida is much different. I clearly know everyone I visit, but someone has to let me know they are in the hospital. I have to keep making myself known to the hospital staff.

We will continue to apply criteria for hospital visiting to the entire range of situations in which hospital visitors find themselves. At this point, clarify your own situation, the setting in which you do your hospital visiting, and have a picture of it before you as you consider your orientation.

Begin by getting to know the people who can help. Cultivate an awareness of different professionals in the hospital system and use them regularly. People to contact are chaplains, social workers, nursing supervisors in particular units or areas, patient services representatives, and information hosts or hostesses.

Getting Oriented   Begin your tour with the information desk. There is generally a separate file for clergy where patients are listed by religious affiliation. Make sure your denomination is listed in a way that is familiar to your congregation. Communicate this listing to the members of your church so they know how to indicate their affiliation when they go to the hospital.

In another chapter we will discuss ways to activate the minister's role in hospital visiting, but here it is important to note that church members need to be made aware of the importance of the clergy file at the hospital. I have had people refuse to fill out a religious preference card at the hospital out of civil liberty convictions. Here I had to point out that filling out this category helps me find them. My denomination, the United Church of Christ, still has people in it who call themselves Congregationalists, from the parent denomination prior to the merger. I alert the hospital to this dual listing and encourage my members to stick with one name or the other, depending on the characteristics of the community.

No matter how good the system, some names never make it to the religious card file. Therefore it is important to have a standing policy whereby members of the church call you when they or other members are in the hospital.

The second item on your tour should be the visiting policy. What are the hospital visiting hours and when does the hospital prefer to have clergy visit? You may have to balance the hospital's preference with your own convictions. Some pastors like to visit in the morning before regular visiting hours. This gives you a certain amount of privacy and freedom from interruptions by other visitors. However, it is also a time that many of the medical procedures are performed and you may be getting in the way of hospital personnel.

Find out when meals are served and avoid them. This is an awkward time for patient and visitor.

There are times, in emergencies and around surgery, that you cannot follow the most convenient schedule for the hospital. Find out in advance how to get in late at night or early in the morning.

The third piece of information you should obtain is how the hospital will get oriented to you. What will you do about identifying yourself? No one really looks like the stereotype of a minister anymore, so you cannot take it for granted that hospital staff will understand why you are walking through their halls. I have met staff who claim they can always spot a minister, but they've never spotted me. Women and younger pastors all have special difficulty being recognized as clergy. But unless you look like Ichabod Crane, even a middle-aged male will not be easily recognized as a minister.

Find out if the hospital requires you to carry or wear some form of official identification. If not, then it will be up to you to identify yourself. If you wear a clerical collar, this is easy. If this is not your denominational tradition, you will have to make clear who you are. It is important to introduce yourself as a minister at the nurse's station at the floor where you visit. Hospitals are concerned about the security of their patients, and personnel appreciate your courtesy in introducing yourself.

It is also important to find out how the hospital expects you to relate to special areas like the intensive care unit or the emergency room. These are areas which have strict prohibitions for general visitors but which allow clergy special privileges. You need to know your rights for these areas, because staff are not always aware of clergy privilege in specific situations. A later chapter describes some of the unique elements of emergency room and intensive care visitation, but you should find out what policies apply to clergy in your first tour.

The Visit   Having completed your tour, you are now ready for visiting hospital patients from your church.

We share here a variety of styles offered by pastors and hospital personnel. You need to decide which of these styles you are comfortable with.

Depending on the situation of your community, it may be worth calling before visiting. In a large church there may always be enough patients in the hospital to make calling ahead unnecessary. If the church is small and the hospital some distance, then call to confirm that your patient is in the hospital. Call the room to find out if the patient has tests or therapy scheduled so you can plan the best time to visit. This also helps the patient order the day in a setting where the patient has little control of life.

Stop at the nurse's station at each floor you visit. Identify yourself and find out if there are any precautions you must take before entering your patient's room. You may also explain to those at the nurse's station that you will be visiting and would like a certain period of privacy. Some clergy carry religious "Do Not Disturb" signs they hang on the door. I prefer just to mention my visit at the desk. Realize too that if your patient has any particular difficulties, you can go to the nurse's station for help. Having stopped there first facilitates receiving help later.

Knock at the patient's room and wait to be invited in.
Hospital patients suffer many indignities. We need not increase
them. A patient may be on a bed pan, in the midst of significant
pain, or may have just gotten a chance to nap. Give the patient a
chance to express personal needs easily.

Don't feel foolish about introducing yourself, especially
if you are from a large church. It is easy for a patient to be
disoriented and not recognize you outside the context of the
church.

Believe it or not, there is division among the ranks of
church professionals as to whether one should sit down in making a
hospital visit. One school of thought states steadfastly that the pastor
should remain standing. The reason for this is to keep the visit short.
Another perspective states just as firmly that one should definitely sit
and be at eye level with a patient while visiting. We favor the latter
point of view, believing enough personnel enter quickly, stare down
at a patient, perform their duties, and then hurry off. In the sit or not
to sit debate one more detail remains. If you do sit, remember to
return the chair to its original place when you leave. Small details
like this make a big difference in a crowded hospital room.

The length of a visit is important. Knowing the
tendency of clergy toward longwindedness, many resources encourage short visits. Hospital personnel remind us that patients are
weak or they would not be in the hospital. However, there is also
the superficiality of the pastor who stands in the doorway, waves a
jolly greeting, offers a quick blessing, and then departs. Have in
mind an idea of a reasonable period of time for a visit before you
enter the room. Take your cues from the patient. If this is a time the
patient really needs to talk, then stay, and listen. Otherwise keep
the visit brief. Common sense is the key.

Speaking of common sense, there is one rule so basic
as to be embarrassing, but which nevertheless deserves a quick
mention. Do not visit the hospital if you have a communicable
disease or are even at the slightest risk of coming down with one.
We all know this, but the workaholic strain in clergy requires this
reminder. It has often been the case that a co-worker has had to
remind me not to visit the hospital on those days when I was
dragging around with a hacking cough or a pre-flu funk. You are
no good to anyone, especially someone sick, in this condition. Send
a card instead.

With all the preliminaries out of the way, it is time to
consider the visit itself. Begin with gentle data gathering. It is
important to let the patient share his condition, even if you have
already received a report from someone else. Let the patient know

you are concerned about him. This means asking more than a conversational "How are you?" without communicating dread or disaster. Queries like "Tell me what brought you here." "How are you feeling right now?" or "How long do you expect to be here?" give you the information you need to begin your care for this patient. You let the patient speak about herself, which may be a significant step in the patient's understanding of her situation.

Another question, "How sick are you?" lets the patient share a feeling as well as a clinical diagnosis. It quickly establishes how much the patient knows of her own condition. There have been times when I was told that a patient did not know of a malignancy. When I have asked such patients how sick they were, they often replied, "I have cancer." It was a relief for them to say it and a welcome opportunity for both of us to deal with their illness realistically.

It is good to compare the response you recieve from the patient to that of medical personnel and even family. Your own plan for pastoral care should take discrepancies into account. This may mean talking further with doctor and family to facilitate communication and hear other concerns.

When the patient describes his condition with technical medical terms, ask the patient to explain them. This can clarify understandings for the patient and you. Verify explanations later to make sure both the patient and you have a correct understanding. The glossary in the back of this book is a reference. Other resources for medical terminology are listed in the annotated bibliography at the end of this chapter. Neither the glossary of this book nor any medical dictionary should be a substitute for gathering complete medical information from a physician.

After you have gathered primary data about the patient's condition, take time to listen to other stories the patient wishes to tell. Resist the temptation to tell of your own hospital tales. Follow the level of disclosure the patient presents. Be careful of denying deep fears and concerns. Hospitals are frightening places. Even a brief visit for a minor illness can be scary. Listen for this concern, and accept it.

A patient in the hospital for a long-term illness has different needs from the short-term patient. If you will be making numerous visits, then it is important to encourage a variety of stories, memories, and topics. With elderly patients, memory is a golden link with life, and it is good to ask about stories of specific times in their lives.

Many of the current resources on wholistic health report the importance of joy and laughter in healing. Here is a place for great sensitivity and balance. Laughter can be for the spirit of the hospital patient what jogging is for the person of good health. Gentle, joyful news and stories are good gifts for any patient. And as with any good thing, there are limits to the benefits of joy and laughter, especially for patients with abdominal sutures.

Having listened to the patient's immediate concerns, it is also important to ask about needs the patient has outside the hospital. Who is taking care of other family members? Are there people at work who need to be contacted? Are there household chores that need to be taken care of? Use the congregation to respond to these needs. Clergy too often take on these tasks themselves, and this is what the church is for.

Find support tasks suitable to the size of your church. Most clergy in this country serve churches of under 200 members. One of the gifts of the small church is the special; personal care that can be given to patients and family in times of illness. These are opportunities for deep sharing between pastor and parishioner and for good churchwide support. The church can be the enabler of truly wholistic care.

In a larger church extended care will have to be structured. Lay care teams let church members share hospital support with staff. Good organization can keep hospital care personal.

It is important to close the visit with a purpose rather than to just act like you have run out of time. Here the question arises: To pray or not to pray?

There is a stereotype of the graduating seminarian as one unwilling, unable, or unprepared to pray at the hospital room. It was true for me, and many journal articles still proclaim it. There is good reason to be somewhat wary of substituting prayer for good pastoral care. We have seen the opposite stereotype, the "pray at the drop of a hat" pastor. We have seen clergy hide behind sanctimonious prayer rather than engage people in honest struggle over painful issues. We have seen glib, self-serving prayers forced upon unconsenting bed-bound victims. Thus I was hesitant to institutionalize prayer into my hospital visits when I began my ministry. For some people an offer to pray was a suggestion that they were dying. Others found it unnatural or intrusive. But I also had to admit that much of my hesitancy was grounded in my own discomfort and uncertainty in offering prayers. My style is informal and the transition into prayer often felt clumsy. As a result I limited my prayers too severely.

In time, people I have visited taught me how to pray and showed me the power of it. The consensus of virtually all clergy surveyed for this study is that the patient should be asked if she wishes a prayer.

The important step is to ask. The patient's condition, situation, and room environment all contribute to whether or not the patient may desire a prayer. But ask, and offer. Clergy roles are confused. Sometimes we feel out of place in a hospital, not knowing what to do when everyone else has a task to perform. Many of us have rebelled against a tradition of piety. Prayer is what we can and should share.

A simple scripture passage often has deep meaning for the hospital patient, and the clergy person should be prepared to offer this as well. This is not a time to preach or evangelize. This is a time for practicing the presence of the Holy Spirit, opening with gentleness this time and place for grace.

Guidelines for hospital prayers and suggested scripture references appear in later chapters. Here it is important to simply remember to offer prayer and scripture to the patient. Pray out of what you have heard in your visit. Offer the hopes and fears through the strength of faith and tradition.

There is one final point to remember about the visit. You have gathered data, listened to the concerns of the patient, found concrete things to do, and offered prayer and scripture. One thing more to remember is to touch the patient. The hospital patient is poked, jabbed, injected, cut open, sewn up, jostled, and inspected. He may feel totally manhandled. But your gentle touch on the hand or cheek can be grace.

Etiquette and Protocol

1. *When others are in the room.* A room full of visitors presents a dilemma when you pay your call. One minister simply says hello and leaves when other visitors are present. His feeling is that the patient with the full room has all the support she needs, and the pastor could better spend time with patients who have no visitors. Other clergy make a point of announcing that they will be visiting other patients, planning to return at a given time. This gives sensitive visitors a suggestion of when they might leave and give pastor and patient some time together. There are others who just join the crowd, dealing with everyone present, and some ask the visitors to leave so the pastor may have some privacy with the patient.

What should you do? Consider the specific situation and your personal style. In order to make your decision, gather specific data. Who are the people in the room? How is the patient feeling, and does he specifically need time with you alone? What are the needs of visiting family members? How will you connect with them?

In a non-critical situation with an easy flow of visitors, the pastor need not add to the crowd. But in difficult times, the patient needs some privacy with the pastor. If it does not come soon, ask for it. I have been in situations where the patient has directly asked her other visitors to leave so we could have some private time. If the patient cannot do this herself and seems to need this, you may be the person to interpret to others the patient's need to have a crowded room cleared out.

Sometimes a family member keeping close contact with the patient needs special attention. To a friend or family member who has been keeping a long vigil, suggest a cup of coffee or a walk together. Or offer your time to visit with the patient as an opportunity for the family member to take a break.

Your knowledge of the hospital can help a family member find the cafeteria or coffee shop. Often a family member is afraid to venture off the patient's floor simply because he does not know how to find these other facilities. Some of the best pastoral care can be done by sharing a meal with the worried companion of the patient.

The issue of the crowded room raises the question of when the pastor makes a crowd. Just as there are times you need privacy with the patient, so there are also times a patient wishes privacy with friends and family. Clergy also need to know when to leave, gracefully.

2. _Visiting a stranger._   There are occasions when you are asked to see someone with whom you have had no previous contact. By this I mean someone not a member of your church. A church member may ask you to visit a friend, or a hospital staff person may say that someone in the next room needs to see a minister.

Again, gather data, first from the referral source. A nurse or staff person may be facing a situation he cannot handle alone. The staff person may be the one needing the visit, so pay attention to what is being said here, and offer to support the staff person in her role. A church member may have the same need in calling you to see his friend. Your church member may need support in a frightening time.

If you visit the patient, determine how much this patient actually wants to see you. Make sure you are not overstepping someone else's pastoral territory. Consider your own time priorities and determine just what kind of commitment you can make to this person. It may be that a brief visit and prayer are all that is needed. If the patient needs more time than you can give, contact those key hospital personnel you met in your orientation tour.

When a church member asks you to visit a friend, be aware of a phenomenon in certain parts of this country where a member of a church sends her pastor to visit a friend who is a member of another church. I had never experienced this in my own background, and I never quite understood why people asked me to do this until another pastor explained this tradition. It is a kind gesture, sort of like sending flowers, and when the patient, the friend of a friend, has no support system, it can be very meaningful. But it becomes ludicrous when three or four friends send their pastors to a common friend who already has his own pastor.

If you have time to call in behalf of your own parishioner, find out if you are really needed, pay your respects and inform your parishioner that you have made your visit. It is simply good time management and good pastoral care not to duplicate efforts unnecessarily.

The final element to consider in looking at all aspects of the hospital visit is the work situation of the doctors and nurses who treat the patient. They are very aware of your role. They appreciate the clergy visit most when the guidelines suggested here are followed. Hospital staff are virtually unanimous in this recommendation that clergy visits not be overlong, that there be some kind of physical touch in a gentle way with the patient, and that a supportive prayer be offered. You should be aware of their work situation.

Any time a person is hospitalized, the patterns of institutionalization develop. Since the patient has little control over his or her environment everyday elements of life take on monumental importance. Times of meals, medication, and therapy are the major organizers of a patient's day. Patients hang onto any word or gesture which suggests information they seek about their own condition or recovery. When a meal is unpleasant, medication late, or an offhand comment is exaggerated, a patient may become depressed, angered, or confused. It is easy for the hospital visitor to be drawn into the patient's institutionalization syndrome if you are not aware of its characteristics and do not understand the structure and routine of a hospital and its staff.

Be aware of the necessary routines of nursing. A floor nurse cannot be the private nurse to any given patient. Even medication which is prescribed PRN (or, as the situation requires) has to be grouped for efficiency.

Sometimes a patient will ask you to call a nurse or will complain to you about the lack of nursing attention received. Always gather data from the nursing station about the situation before you intervene in the nurse-patient relationship. There may be times when you can facilitate better understanding between the patient and nursing staff, but do not ever try to do this prematurely, that is, before you have taken time to fully understand the situation.

You can be most helpful to the patient if you clearly understand the nursing routine, shift schedules, and nursing plan for this patient. You can interpret these to the patient. In so doing, you may develop a deeper empathy for the role of the nursing staff as well. Use this empathy to be a supportive member of the health care team in the hospital.

Realize too that there will be times that the nursing staff needs your support. The serious illness, pain, and even death of patients they care for affects their lives deeply. Be sensitive to the times they need help.

For doctors, time is the key issue. The average internist in private practice, for example, has eight to ten patients in the hospital. The internist is aware that he or she has a coordinating, interpreting role to the patient. The physician will often take a pulse and listen with a stethoscope primarily to make physical contact with the patient. The doctor will reinterpret comments of a surgeon or other specialist and listen to the patient's concerns. Sometimes emergencies will prevent the internist from seeing a patient on a certain day, and this may be upsetting to the patient. Doctors consistently cite the difficulty of finding time to keep up the human contact with the patient while going about professional duties as the key pressure of their job.

You as clergy can relate to this doctor by understanding just how he or she needs your support. Some doctors welcome a ten minute break over a cup of coffee, just to unwind. Others will tell you they would rather have the extra time with patients and prefer that you not try to make them take a break. Find out from the physicians treating patients you see how you can best support them in their role.

Your empathy with the situation of the doctor and nurse will enhance your total hospital ministry. You will be trusted by hospital staff. You will be able to communicate the needs and role of the hospital staff to the patient. And when necessary, the hospital staff will listen to your concerns on behalf of the patient.

Consulting With the Physician

How will you know when you should consult with the physician about the patient's condition? Generally, you can rely on the family to share with you what has been reported by the physician. If it's comfortable for the family, be there when they meet with the physician, so you can hear what they have been told and be identified to the physician as a significant support person to the family. Contacts with the physician beyond these times should be for specific reasons, such as an agitated family member, organ donations, and preferences regarding extraordinary treatment interventions. You receive your authority in these areas from the family.

One of the areas in which clergy and patients often feel uncomfortable is getting a second opinion for a medical procedure. A patient or family may fear that this will offend their physician. However, second opinions, especially in serious interventions such as surgery, are becoming routine. Some industries which partially provide workers' health insurance discount costs to the employee when a second opinion is sought. Health care providers should respect the right of individuals to this type of consultation. Usually it is wise to notify the original physician of this second consultation. Often this physician can facilitate referral to a competent colleague. At the very least, the pastor can alleviate any feelings of guilt or disloyalty the parishioner may have in seeking a second opinion. Such a consultation is a wise and increasingly routine procedure.

You now have the basic map for orientation to the hospital, making your call or visit, and dealing with some of the special issues of the patient's environment. With this information, it is up to you to develop your own unique style. Pastors who shared data for this chapter each prefer different times to visit. One finds non-visiting hours to his liking. Another sees the mid-afternoon as the time a patient is most free of other procedures. One pastor makes a point of visiting late in the evening the night before surgery, a time when a patient often feels most alone. That same pastor by the way also added, "I never bring the altar flowers."

How you use this information is up to you. Now we move on the more specific situations.

Bibliography

Biegert, John E. *Looking Up While Lying Down.* New York: Pilgrim, 1983.

Clinebell, Howard. *Basic Types of Pastoral Counselling.* Nashville, Tn.: Abingdon, reissued 1984.

Nelson, James B. *Rediscovering the Person in Medical Care: Patient, Family, Physician; Nurse, Chaplain, Pastor.* Minneapolis, Mn.: Augsburg, 1976.
Essays on identity of persons involved in health care, providing opportunities for understanding and care of all parties in the hospital setting.

Pipe, John H. "From Brokeness to Wholeness." *Minister—A Journal of the American Baptist Ministers Council.* Valley Forge, Pa. Vol. V(1), Spring 1984, pp. 1–3, 13–15. John Pipe shares his experience of long term hospitalization following a car accident that left him partially paralyzed. This is an excellent account of the experience of hospitalization from the perspective of one who has also been a visiting pastor.

Medical Dictionaries

Mosby's Medical and Nursing Dictionary. St. Louis, Mo.: C.V. Mosby Co.
Physician's Desk Reference 38th edition. Oradell, N.J.: Medical Economics Co., Inc., 1984.
Stedman's Medical Dictionary. Baltimore, Md.: Williams and Wilkins.
Taber's Cyclopedic Medical Dictionary. Philadelphia: F.A. Davis Co.

All of these dictionaries offer definitions of medical terms and diseases. Some are more helpful in certain fields than others. The *Physician's Desk Reference* is the most well-known and is available in most public libraries.

The Minister is a Team Member   3
Getting Into the Game

Activating the Role of Minister There are at least three dimensions involved in the pastor's enactment of this role with hospitalized parishioners. Each is important and related to the other. The first dimension can be referred to as preparatory in nature, the second is the act of taking initiative, and the third focuses the actual provision of care.

Preparing to be pastor when parishioners are hospitalized involves two efforts: an educational process for the congregation, and the continuing professional development of the minister. In the life of the congregation, there can be concentrated emphases during which the pastor and other resource persons provide information about the health care field, perhaps lay ministry, and certainly the role of pastoral ministry during the crisis of illness. It has been mentioned several times already how important this type of preparation can be for persons who have never experienced hospitalization. Some of the information shared in chapter two can be useful. Equally important would be utilizing a panel of resource persons from local hospitals to address key issues. Examples of topics which could compose an emphasis week might include:

1. Patient-physician relationships
2. Informed consent and decision making
3. Living wills and natural death acts
4. Bereavement and survivorship

5. Coping with illness in the family
6. Faith and wholeness during illness
7. Patient and family concerns during illness

Forming a health care cabinet in the church could provide a central lay focus to bring before the congregation pertinent issues. It would certainly be possible for such a group to address preventive as well as crisis issues.

A central portion of this preparatory phase is for the congregation to understand what the pastor can offer during illness and hospitalization and how the resources of the congregation may be utilized to provide added support. During illness, the pastoral role is experienced in many ways. Clarifying a hierarchy of needs is often part of an initial assessment visit. Much of this is accomplished through listening to what has led to hospitalization and how the experience has been to date. Providing basic support is essential, just being there and caring while at the same time symbolically representing the love of God. The sharing of scripture, communion (if appropriate), and prayer constitutes a sacramental ministry. On other occasions, counseling which refocuses values, assists decision making, affirms relationship is important. The congregation can benefit from discussion of the pastoral role prior to a crisis. It informs them regarding the functions of ministry and aids in removing any sense of awkwardness about the minister's visits.

Each congregation must decide how to organize itself for providing care during a member's illness. This deciding and any subsequent revisions of the plan are best accomplished prior to crisis moments. A health care council can provide scenarios to which any action plan can be theoretically applied in an effort to test out how well an organizational scheme might work. Any plan must contain both spiritual and concrete services. Prayer, for example, is a comforting notion to patients, especially when they know an entire congregation is participating. It is also useful to have persons who know that a prepared meal or mown grass will be a welcome sight. Nor will anything more quickly spoil the good intentions of a caring congregation than a patient-family who receive ten phone calls a day inquiring as to current status. One person can be appointed as the communications link. A similar role can be reserved for another person to serve as "gatekeeper" on bedside visitation. The only thing worse than a perpetually ringing phone is an endless string of visitors, all of whom expect the patient to be glad to see them, as if the event had been planned with the visitors in mind!

A recently hospitalized patient counted the number of persons entering her room each day. [1] The daily average was fifty-six. This included staff as well as personal friends. Nevertheless, think of how you would respond to having even two unscheduled visitors to your home on a day when you felt great.

Obviously a careful balance is required, lest the patient feel abandoned or forgotten. Some churches divide members into networks to provide support. This model allows for a rotating coordinator who can delegate responsibilities.

The pastor's preparation is also ongoing. An excellent approach, perhaps the best, is an opportunity to be a part of a Clinical Pastoral Education program.[2] If C.P.E. is unavailable to you, there are other ways to grow as a helping person during life crises. A senior minister who is willing to be a mentor, such as was mentioned in the introduction, is one alternative. More formal structures might involve contracting with a chaplain, pastoral counselor, social worker, psychiatric nurse, marriage and family therapist, mental health professional, psychologist, or other persons trained in counseling, to periodically review your interpersonal interactions with parishioners. Special workshops are available, usually for a nominal registration fee, as are books written to enhance understanding from the pastor's perspective. The important thing is to view yourself as being in the process of learning, to have a learning plan, and to enlist the support of your congregation in supporting your efforts, with both time and budget. It is easy to demonstrate that every professional caregiver group has requirements for continuing education.

In addition to preparation, the second aspect of implementing the pastoral role is the act of initiative. In normal parish life, the minister is often needful of opportunities for either anonymity or temporary relief from being "on duty." The positive side of this constant spotlight is that s/he doesn't have to spend any significant time contesting the role. Entering the hospital, however, is yet another matter. At worst, it is as if all the status and recognition in the parish gets left at the hospital information desk. In the minister's accustomed place stands the physician. Consequently,

---

1. "Too Many Visitors" in "Shop Talk," *The Wall Street Journal*, May 31, 1984, p. 33.
2. For more information about available programs in your area, write: Association for Clinical Pastoral Education, 475 Riverside Drive, New York, New York 10115.

initiative is called for in a unique way to assume the role as pastor. The responsibility is always there to define who you are, what you are doing, and to be persuasive enough to enlist hospital staff's cooperation. This is not comfortable, although it is a challenge. The inadequate solution is to capitulate to an awkward system in the name of a busy schedule, slip into the patient's room, pray, and then leave. Initiative, however, can lead to a team membership and is to be equated with assertiveness, not aggressive behavior, though it may on occasion feel like the latter. In hospitals where chaplains are employed or where a C.P.E. program exists, some of this ground may have been plowed for you. If not, perhaps the local Ministerial Association can devise a project to improve working relationships between ministers and hospitals.

The provision of pastoral care, the third dimension of role enactment, is the most difficult to discuss. Perhaps the best contribution which a book such as this can make is to frame several crucial issues in providing care. It is not uncommon for ministers to be impressed to the point of intimidation at how concrete and measurable are the tasks performed by most health professionals. In an effort to compensate, I have seen pastors become activists in hospital visitation, expressing anxiety through attempts at humor, taking the patient's dirty laundry home to be washed, or going to the gift shop to purchase a newspaper. These activities generally suggest a lack of clarity in pastoral identity, heightened somewhat by the loss of status and the skilled tasks performed by others. Simply being there as a concerned, caring person does not feel adequate. But it often is.

Few people enter the patient's room with the task of sitting and listening to them. Yet feelings and concerns, values, self-image, and faith issues are a storm inside, needing to be shared. This is the strength of the pastoral role—to be able to sit and listen with understanding. The patient needs to feel blessed by feeling enough worth that someone would be concerned to hear what the illness experience is like. Self-worth that is normally defined by doing or productivity is unavailable to the patient. Discovering worth in simply being is elusive, until you have the experience of being listened to, with its attendant emotions of being accepted and forgiven.

This skill of listening is hard work, because when done well, the ear is informed by good counseling skills, relevant knowledge, and the wisdom of faith. It is a most active process. At the end of the day, however, the minister cannot count incisions, stiches, or medicines prescribed to measure worth. Being clear about the pastoral role is crucial to the enactment of it, particularly during crisis experiences.

Understanding the Organization of the Hospital The hospital exists in order to provide care for ill persons who cannot be treated on an ambulatory or outpatient basis. A few services, such as the various clinics and departments like radiology, will serve both outpatients and inpatients. Within the institution, one researcher has estimated that over 230 different professional disciplines provide direct or indirect services to patients.[3] Some of these disciplines will have personal contact with the patient while others will play a crucial role but never see or even know the patient's name. The physician's diagnosis, for example, was probably confirmed by a lab technologist who also tested for the drug producing the most beneficial response. Yet the patient will not likely know of this person who played such an important role in treatment.

The hospital is organized so that these multiple professions can effectively work together. The aim of each profession is excellence in patient care, but this term "excellence" does not always mean the patient is as comfortable as if s/he were at home. Data must be collected prior to physician rounds, which may mean bathing a patient, changing bed covers, or taking vital signs at 6:00 A.M. Napping patients are often wakened. None of these inconveniences mean the hospital's organization does not serve the patient well. In fact, they are designed for efficiency which, one hopes, lowers the cost of care. For example, it is not pleasant for a patient to wait an extended time for an x-ray or a CAT scan. However, these machines are incredibly expensive and maximizing procedures lowers unit costs. Keeping the machine "waiting" increases costs. These savings are reflected in the patient's bill.

Hospitals functionally organize and schedule activities as if the health care professionals employed there, particularly physicians, were the primary consumers. These professionals attempt to reflect to administration the specific needs they frequently hear expressed by their patients. These express needs, in time, become part of the hospital routine. Examples of such innovations are birthing centers and the availability of gourmet meals. If you have been a hospital patient recently, undoubtedly you were asked to complete an evaluative questionnaire. These efforts reflect the desire of hospitals to please patients, encouraging a return visit should another hospitalization be required.

---

3. Stanley J. Reiser, M.D., "Institutional Ethics Committees and Healthcare Decisionmaking," American Society of Law & Medicine Conference, Houston, Texas, Feb. 23–24, 1984.

In a community hospital physician rounds will usually occur early in the morning and late in the afternoon. Most of the daytime hours are reserved for the particular practice of the physician, in his office or perhaps in surgery. In referral and research centers, most often located adjacent to university settings, schedules may vary considerably from the traditional community hospital. This is because the practice of the medical staff is usually confined to hospital and clinic patients. Another difference in the community hospital is that the patient will usually know his physician, perhaps from previous office visits, and this physician may be the only M.D. he encounters during hospitalization. At the research setting, however, the primary or attending physician will make almost all decisions but will not be among the M.D.'s most often seen by the patient. Day to day care will be provided by house staff composed of fellows, residents, and medical students. Because of their availability, consultants from other medical specialties may also be frequently utilized. Initially this can be confusing to a patient, particularly as they learn that medical specialists in different fields can have varying opinions in diagnosing or treating an illness.

During the early morning physician rounds, orders for the day's care plan may be continued or altered. Specific tests or treatments may be ordered and scheduled. Through most of the morning and into the mid-afternoon these tests will be completed. Late afternoon physician rounds will integrate results into the care plan and perhaps alter treatment to reflect what has been learned. The pastor who plans to visit a hospitalized parishioner will do well to reserve the later afternoon for his visit as well. The likelihood of finding the patient in is increased, as is the possibility of being there during the physician rounds. In one sense, late afternoon represents the end of the patient's "workday." Tests and procedures are tiring and anxiety-producing. The opportunity to reflect and make a transition into the evening can be a welcome respite which can provide a warm reception to the sensitive pastor.

Almost all hospitals will organize their inpatient areas according to major medical disciplines. This allows nursing staff, in particular, to concentrate skills according to patient needs. An illustrative listing of medical disciplines would include the following, with specialties in each area:

Anesthesiology
Community Health and
Family Medicine
Medicine
  Allergy-rheumatology
  Cardiology

Dermatology
Endocrinology
Gastroenterology
Hematology

Medicine (continued)
  Infectious diseases
  Nephrology
  Oncology
  Pulmonary
Neurology
Obstetrics and Gynecology
Pathology
Pediatrics
  Adolescent medicine
  Cardiology
  Endocrinology
  Gastroenterology
  Genetics
  Hematology
  Immunology
  Infectious diseases

Neonatology
Oncology
Pulmonary
Renal-urology
Psychiatry
  Adult
  Adolescent
  Child
Radiology
Surgery
  General
  Neurological
  Orthopaedic
  Otolaryngology
  Pediatric
  Plastic and reconstructive
  Thoracic and cardiovascular
  Urology

Medicine, Neurology, Obstetrics and Gynecology, Pediatrics, Psychiatry, and Surgery will have hospital beds assigned to their service. As mentioned earlier, these beds will usually be grouped together by general area or specialty so that nursing staff and others who have been trained to care for the special needs are also clustered. Anesthesiology, Pathology, and Radiology may serve the hospitalized patient, but do not have assigned beds as such. Generally, Anesthesiology may provide medical supervision in Intensive Care Units. Community Health and Family Medicine extends care through hospital outpatient clinics and satellite clinics located in rural areas. For the visiting pastor, knowledge of which medical service the parishioner is on will provide initial clues to the nature of the health problem.

In addition, special units exist which concentrate services for patients who are critically ill. One grouping of special areas is called "Intensive Care Units." They may be designated as surgical, medical, pediatric, burn, coronary, or neonatal intensive care. The patients in such units are critically ill and require both regular staff intervention as well as close technical monitoring. Changes in the patient's condition are determined by the minute and hour, which is largely unlike patients in other areas of the hospital. In I.C.U. areas, the nursing staff to patient ratio will usually be 1:1 or 2. For family, visiting hours in these units are generally restricted to short periods of ten to fifteen minutes each visit. Many hospitals will permit the minister to visit at times other than visiting hours. If this is not the case in your area, a meeting between your Ministerial Association and a representative of the hospital can aid in developing a mutually agreeable policy. It is important not to take away from the family visiting time.

Upon entering the hospital, the pastor should learn from the admissions area where the parishioner is located by room number or special unit. This Information Desk will be coordinated usually by an employee or the Hospital Auxiliary, a volunteer organization serving the institution. When arriving at the patient's floor or unit, it is often wise to stop first at the nursing station, identify yourself and ask to speak to the nurse who is working with the patient that day. Each floor or unit will have a nursing supervisor as well as nurses who are assigned to a particular patient. From this assigned nurse, the pastor can learn information which might aid in shaping the visit. A restless night of sleeping, a particularly rigorous procedure, or a lot of visitors can render the patient too exhausted to sustain a lengthy or lighthearted visit. Other health professionals who might assist the pastor in this regard are the chaplain, social worker, or patient representative. The key ingredient is that the minister take the initiative to meet these people and regularly utilize them during the parishioner's hospitalization. These contacts can be invaluable and time-saving. For example, arriving at the patient's room to find her off the floor at x-ray can initially feel like a wasted visitation effort. However, an acquaintance with the chaplain can often result in an escort to the x-ray area. Moreover, this can be an excellent time for a patient visit and save the pastor the time of a return effort.

The same nurse will not always work with a patient throughout hospitalization. It is always true that at least two different nurses will be involved with the patient each day. Nursing shifts are traditionally divided into three eight hour periods, daytime (7:00 A.M.–3 P.M.), evening (3:00 P.M.–11 P.M.), and night (11:00 P.M.–7 A.M.). A new scheduling format is called "seven on–seven off." Monday through Friday, the nurse works eight hour shifts, and on Saturday-Sunday, works twelve hours each day. The Saturday-Sunday hours qualify as overtime plus bonus, which equates to an eighty-hour time period. Instead of working the second week, the R.N. has "seven off." One result of this is a more stable nursing work force. For the longer term patient, it can mean adjusting to new nurses more frequently. The visiting pastor, as well, must not grow comfortable relating to a particular nurse. It will be necessary to reacquaint with new nurses regularly. Consistency in personnel will more likely be found in the chaplain, social worker, or patient representative.

The most important organizational member of the health care team for the visiting pastor is the patient. Although many persons are not aware of their full rights, the patient is a partner in the health care arena. And the patient is a powerful partner. When of legal age and competent, no decision can be made, treatment begun or changed apart from the patient's consent. Moreover, decisions by the patient must reflect "informed consent." Technically, this notion of informed consent implies that the patient receives more than a warning of inherent risks. Information should describe alternative treatments and in a clear enough fashion that lifestyle projections can be made for each possible choice.

Another very important dimension of the patient's power is in structuring his own team members. The hospital meets the patient with a group of professionals who are generally familiar with one another's function and who, as needed, will serve the patient. At the same time, the patient brings to the hospital a team of associates and helpers who must be integrated into the care plan. It is the responsibility of the patient to do this. Literally, the patient has the power to exclude or include anyone, including family members, from visiting and having information regarding diagnosis and prognosis. Among these team members brought into the hospital by the patient is the pastor. From the perspective of the hospital's legal concern, all rights and privileges held by the minister have been bequeathed by the patient. It can be helpful if, early in the hospitalization experience, the patient clarifies to the physician and staff which team members compose his partnership. During the regular life of the congregation, the minister can find ways to educate parishioners to this aspect of their role when they are a patient. A vital link is missing for the patient's team members as well, when the patient cannot assume, for whatever reasons, a partnership role.[4]

When the pastor enters the hospital, s/he should assume the attitude of being a member of the health care team. Apart from that attitude, s/he becomes only a religious functionary, putting in an appearance which plays no significant role in the care plan for the patient. This attitude on the part of the minister is realistic if homework is done to educate the parishioner to the dimension of

4.   Norman Cousins, *Anatomy of an Illness*, New York: W.W. Norton and Co., Inc., 1979.

partnership in being a patient, if the pastor is prepared to be part of the patient's team, and if initiative is taken to meet and work with the hospital team of professionals. Underlying this basic right of team membership is the rich historical tradition of ministry to those who are ill, and the role of faith in health and wholeness. The history of the church affirms this role.

Various Types of Health Care Settings   Comments need to be made about the different kinds of hospitals and helping institutions you might encounter as a pastor. My work has occurred almost exclusively in the setting of a major university health center. This kind of hospital is a tertiary level referral facility, which generally means that patients have either unusual illnesses or ones less frequently encountered, or that special technical knowledge or equipment is needed for treatment. Both of these characteristics are often the case. Moreover, the patient usually comes for hospitalization some distance from home and familiar support systems. To stand in our lobby and overhear the comments by patients and families upon their arrival is to be reminded of what an overwhelming experience it is to come to our place.

In some cases our health center has an employee population that exceeds that of the patient's home town. Some ride an elevator for the first time. Our hallways buzz with traffic, and there are so many people involved in the care of the patient that knowing who his doctor is can be quite confusing, even if he has the person's name. In this type of environment a pastor can enter the hospital, go to a patient's floor, complete the visit, leave, and no one seems to notice. If you activate your role as has been discussed in another section, you will have to assert yourself amid all this busyness.

In many private hospitals, however, you will enter what might seem, in comparison, to be a hallowed environment. Hallways, particularly in patient care areas, are relatively empty. People talk in hushed tones. And you stand out immediately as someone who doesn't work there. In fact, before you go very far, someone will probably stop you and inquire if they can help you. In more rural communities, your role as pastor may make you a known entity and most persons will automatically assist you in whatever way possible.

Children's hospitals may seem to have more of a community spirit and organization about them. There will be game rooms and play areas. Resident teachers may be on the staff to assist children to remain current with their assignments. Some hospitals provide a sleep-in arrangement for a parent in the child's room. There may be parent support groups, such as at Norton Children's Hospital in Louisville, Kentucky. The atmosphere is structured but may seem less formal. This is communicated in part by the fact that nursing staff will frequently wear uniforms in pastel colors, not white, so as to make the children more comfortable.

Specialty facilities like psychiatric hospitals and substance abuse rehabilitation centers present a quite different environment. These facilities structure a milieu which is part of the patient's therapy. For example, in the psychiatric hospital, the patient may be assigned duties which involve some work-related activities. Individual and group therapy as well as activity periods are scheduled several times weekly. Social outings and meals are often planned as a group activity. In light of the schedule being a part of the therapeutic environment, the pastor should call the facility prior to a visit and perhaps speak to the patient's physician about how to best complement the patient's treatment. Should a visit be appropriate it will usually be scheduled for a set time. If that is not appropriate, there are other supportive activities which the pastor can do. These concerns are discussed in greater detail in Chapter 5 under "Psychiatric Hospitalization."

It is not an understatement to say that all hospitals are not the same. The pastor will prepare better for a visit if this fact is acknowledged and some effort is made to understand the nature of each institution where visits might occur. These differences will often provide explicit direction as to how much initiative the pastor must assert, how much planning must go into a visit, or whether a visit is appropriate at all. Equally as important is that understanding the nature of the setting will help guide the pastoral concerns which might be present. Although this book cannot accomplish such a comprehensive review of each type of setting, let me discuss one institution not yet mentioned.

The nursing home facility will probably increase in frequency as the target for pastoral visits. It is very helpful if you understand its uniqueness.[5]

a. The *core* endeavor of the nursing facility is not health care, but custodial care. Health care is the specialty of the hospital.

---

5. J. Lynn, "Institutional Ethics Committees and Healthcare Decisionmaking." American Society of Law & Medicine Conference, Houston, Texas, Feb. 23–24, 1984.

b. Custodial care has its central foci, food, clothing, and shelter.
c. Most of the nursing homes are "mom and pop" operations with a growing interest on the part of for-profit chains and religiously sponsored groups.
d. The median stay is long-term, defined as greater than one year in length.
e. Staff in these facilities is dominated by non-physicians, usually a director of nursing or an administrator. Federal programs such as Medicare require a once-a-month contact between physician and patient. Most medical contact is "continue current plan" and if a patient worsens, then a move to a hospital is initiated.
f. Most patients will die at the nursing home facility.
g. Treatment goals largely center around maintaining a patient, with a slow decline, while keeping them comfortable.
h. A history of abuse and/or scandal results in it being difficult to hire good employees.
i. Funding is from predominantly Federal sources and their regulations for care provide most standards of care.
j. Patients usually have little choice whether or not they are there and it is not unusual for families to be either remote or not closely involved in care.

Despite an initial impression in reading this list that nursing homes are despicable places, there are many model programs which are emerging to change the historic image into one of care and not neglect. A careful reading between the lines would suggest many themes for pastoral concern. Loneliness, rejection, a sense of failure, loss overload, increasing limitations, isolation, fear, suffering, and dependency would represent just a few. An in-depth understanding of the purposes and goals of institutions in your community would obviously aid you in giving depth to your role in that setting. That information is best gained by meeting with some of the key personnel from these institutions.

Rights, Privileges, and Functions   The enactment of ministry is ultimately grounded in the sense of calling and vocation which is experienced by the pastor throughout a career. The validity of this commitment becomes clearer as the years pass, and a look over the shoulder confirms what one, by faith, believes to be God's will for the future. Along the way, however, concrete passages occur which bestow functional rights and privileges to the minister. Even those denominational traditions which require no educational credentials insist upon a "call" and will necessitate at least one congregation confirming the candidates' experience before granting ordination. It is still true that the training of ministers, physicians, and lawyers is regarded as professional and not academic in nature, as defined by a university.

In the public and private sector, however, the minister's rights and privileges are recognized in the context of a relationship with a specific church and more importantly, with a particular parishioner, who regards the minister as pastor. Hospitals follow the wishes of the patient-family. The pastor is welcome in the hospital, even in areas where friends of the family are not permitted, such as Intensive Care areas. This welcome is usually a part of the hospital Policy and Procedure manual, and is not questioned until the patient indicates a concern or expresses negative feelings about the relationship.

The rights and privileges extended to the pastor by the hospital are special. Access to the patient at other than regular visiting hours is permitted. If staff is aware of the minister's visit, efforts will be made to provide privacy. Rituals of faith are deemed not only theologically important, but as being of comfort, providing a sense of peace and well-being. Many staff are aware that illness is a "teachable" moment in life and thoughtful review of values, priorities, and use of personal energy can result in a more healthy and purposeful orientation during and following recovery. This privilege of being welcome in the hospital is quite unique among professional care givers. Few, if any other, professionals are welcomed in all parts of the hospital. This fact is very important to remember. A nurse from a surgical unit will be gently "challenged" should s/he appear on a medical floor. Similarly, an M.D. will not be welcome in the room of another M.D.'s patient unless formally consulted to render a professional opinion. Yet the pastor's presence in any hospital unit will be viewed as appropriate and customary.

Complementary to the welcome afforded a pastor in the hospital is the function of taking initiative. When the minister learns of a parishioner's hospitalization, there is no quiet waiting for an invitation to visit or to consult. The pastor goes to the hospital and establishes direct contact with the patient and/or family as soon as reasonably possible. It is the right to take initiative toward those who are needful which is a uniqueness in the pastoral role. In some situations, the minister is wise to behave as do some other professionals, and wait for a parishioner to call for an appointment. During crises, however, the pastor almost always takes initiative and becomes involved prior to being called.

Consequently, when the pastor enters the hospital, the welcome afforded is a privilege associated with role and function. Stopping by the nursing station is not for the purpose of "asking permission" to see the patient. To the contrary, that right is not up for debate, with the exception of psychiatric hospitalization. Touching base with hospital staff serves several helpful purposes. First, it activates the minister's role as a member of the health care team. Team members do not function in isolation. Secondly, hospital staff will know if this is a good time to visit the patient. For example, do you waken a sleeping patient? Information from the nurse that the patient "had a difficult night" or "she has been anxious to see you all day" provides helpful direction. Otherwise, a categorical rule never to waken sleeping patients might result in frustration to both parishioner and pastor.

The functions of ministry during the crisis of illness and hospitalization utilize almost all of the pastor's skills. A possible exception is that of proclamation or preaching, although in longer-term hospitalizations or convalescence the ability of cassette recordings from the church's worship services can be comforting. As a function of quality assurance, many chaplains measure types of interventions with patients. Usually, these interventions are descriptive of pastoral functions. Examples of these are:

A.   *Type of visit*

1. New admission
2. Follow-up visit
3. Pre-surgical
4. Family centered
5. Staff consultation
6. Discharge planning

B.   *Purpose of visit*

1. Supportive
2. Sacerdotal
3. Ethical
4. Counseling
5. Long-term
6. Terminal

Having a plan in mind for the intent/purpose of your visit, with a backdrop of what type it is, can lend shape to an experience that can, at times, feel too unstructured. However, any plans as to the intent must be held tentatively. A follow-up visit, for example, where you wish to explore issues as a counselor might find the patient exhausted and able to use only brief support and/or a prayer (sacerdotal). The sensitive pastor will be aware of these various ways of functioning, and like a good shepherd, call upon the necessary and appropriate skills for providing care.

Community   It is easy to become a "Lone Ranger" in ministry. The
Resources   profession of ministry lends itself to individuality, if
not isolation. Therefore, it is important to develop systems and structures which can work against the natural tendency toward isolation. In the field of hospital visitation, one way of avoiding the Lone Ranger syndrome is to become familiar with and involved in resources in the community which can enhance your hospital ministry.

The first resource is other clergy. A good support group of other ministers, whether that be one or two friends or an organized group which regularly meets for sharing, is an essential base for ministry in general. It can help you with specific issues and concerns surrounding hospital visitation. You can share visitation responsibilities during vacations. You can consult when you are unsure of what kind of support the patient needs. You can even present specific case studies for the kind of feedback that can sharpen your skills. Most of all, you can be good mutual support for each other in difficult times. Just as lay visitation groups need mutual support, so ministers need consultation and support with each other as well.

Second, make contact with a representative cross-section of the medical community. Take time to find out what kind of assistance the medical people in your congregation can offer when you need clarification of a parishioner's medical problems. Then supplement that help with communication with other medical professionals. Find doctors who will explain diseases and procedures which are unfamiliar to you.

Third, become familiar with the hospice program in your community. Hospice is a nationwide movement to provide assistance to the terminally ill and their families. Hospices exist in different forms throughout the country. All, however, are autonomous programs of coordinated in- and outpatient services. The hospice operates on many levels. It is interdisciplinary, using a wide spectrum of health care and community professionals. The hospice often has a chaplain or a counselor on its staff, but these people do not try to take the place of the individual's pastor. The hospice is often a clearing house for services.

The hospice works to help families treat their loved ones at home as long as it is possible and desirable. Personnel related to the hospice teach families skills such as how to give medication, or turn the patient, encouraging families to do as much as they can in the home. Often it may be just one simple way of making a patient more comfortable that a hospice worker provides, and this seems to make all the difference. The hospice also helps families find nurses who will do home duty, refers them to counselors and social workers as needed, and provides a general umbrella of support through the illness.

There are 2,000 hospices nationally. If you cannot find a hospice through your local hospital, call an oncologist, a cancer specialist. This doctor can usually put you in touch with the closest hospice. If a hospice does not exist in or near your community, consider starting one. This is an excellent program for a church to initiate. Once begun, it becomes self-sufficient.

The hospice uses all levels of professional medical personnel as well as volunteers from the community. Usually a referral to a hospice must come from a medical doctor. The physical needs of the patient and the emotional needs of the family are all considered by hospice personnel. This is an invaluable community resource.

Fourth, it has been mentioned before to contact the chaplain or department of pastoral care at any hospitals which have them. Work with the hospital chaplain to determine how best to use his or her assistance.

Fifth, become familiar with your community mental health center. Take time to meet with the director so you understand the mental health care system and so the director knows who you are. If possible, make contact with a psychiatrist as well. Both are good resources for referral and supervision.

Finally, be aware of whatever is available in terms of specialized health clinics. Planned Parenthood, county health departments, private emergency centers and other organizations like them often play an important part in the health care of a community. The minister should be familiar with the services they offer.

The best time to make these contacts is when you first arrive at a community. You are new, and it is natural to introduce yourself to other professionals at this time. If it is more comfortable, make these contacts when you have a particular need, such as a patient seeking hospice care. Take the time to let the professionals know who you are so that the next contact will be easier.

Whether you are in a large or small church in an urban or rural setting, it is important to develop networks of support and information among the different resources in the community. You can minister more effectively in a community where you know who can help you and your parishioners in time of need. Likewise, you will be respected and will receive the best assistance when other medical professionals recognize your desire to be knowledgeable in the resources the community has to offer.

Chaplain-Pastor Collaboration

The pastor and chaplain have many reasons for working closely together. Each can potentially discover in the other a colleague for mutual support and understanding. The chaplain usually needs this linkage because denominational structures may not adequately relate to a person in specialized ministry. A classic problem for both chaplains and parish ministers is that each needs a pastor. Both might discover such a need fulfilled in the other. The pastor can often find a resource in the focused interpersonal skills of the chaplain, which can enhance enactment of pastoral tasks as well as provide an educational resource for the congregation. Finally, while the chaplain is often able to facilitate a pastor's involvement in hospital, it is always the Church and the pastor's faithful work which legitimizes the presence of the chaplain in the larger community.

During the crisis of illness there is a more intense need to work together. Although the roles of the pastor and chaplain may appear to be similar, they are more often complementary in nature. For example, the hospital chaplain's specialized task is to assist and support the patient/family through the experience of a life crisis. Even in cases where the illness is chronic in nature and necessitates repeated hospitalizations, the patient-chaplain relationship is punctuated by lapses in time and remains rather singleminded in its focus. The pastor on the other hand lives in the community with the patient/family. If involved in their lives, the pastor has a more rich exposure to and familiarity with them. He or she will know of the individual's career dreams and aspirations, school experiences, marital struggles, and perhaps attend the same social events. The full range of spiritual and family life will be the focus. The chaplain may be an expert in crisis ministry, but it is the pastor who will live in and around the patient/family for an extended period. As such the pastor may literally have "layers" of experiences involving the patient while the chaplain has a more singular involvement.

If the pastor utilizes the chaplain's insights and under-standings of the illness experience, the chaplain needs to realize that this sharing occurs because the pastor will often be the primary caregiver. When the patient faces discharge, hospital staff will frequently realize that a referral service for follow-up is needed. At times, especially in rural communities, the minister is the only available helping resource. If you combine this with what well might be a minister's lifelong knowledge of the patient then the chaplain should make every effort to involve the pastor in patient care consultations. In like manner, the pastor should not overlook this special resource. Sharing this knowledge in an appropriate manner which serves the parishioner is a further enactment of the pastor's role in hospital ministry.

There are multiple examples of the benefit this kind of consultation can bring to the patient/family. While hospitalized for a hernia repair, a middle-aged man suffered the loss of his wife due to a massive stroke. This occurred several days prior to discharge. It was a minister from his community who "caught" this grief-stricken man as a result of a thoughtful referral. In a less dramatic but equally important case, a pastor phoned the hospital chaplain to share insights into a parishioner's religious attitudes. As a result the chaplain was able to more individually "tailor" the rituals of faith to provide comfort and support. In another case, hospital staff became frustrated with a family's interaction during a patient's hospitalization. Each family member seemed to be taking sides against one another to the detriment of the patient's sense of well-being. Their pastor was able to assist the staff in understanding how the illness crisis had rekindled an old family feud, and together they were able to join ranks and realign the family to become part of the process of the patient getting well.

The pastor should view the work of the chaplain as an extension of the church's ministry, especially in a highly specialized sense. Because of the chaplain's focused expertise, the pastor might learn of dimensions in the patient/family which can more clearly direct his or her ministry. All this should occur, however, in the larger context of the community where the patient lives and works. As a vital part of that community, the pastor and the church are an important context where much of what has been learned during illness will be integrated into faith and life. For the pastor, it is not simply a matter of getting the parishioner back into normal routines. After the experience of illness, few people are ever the same again. They view the world and their place in it differently. The chaplain may help the patient identify the process of these changes, but is the pastor who guides the patient/family into a meaningful reorganization of beliefs and understandings. Together, the chaplain and pastor form a good team if consultation and collaboration occur.

Bibiliography

Butler, R.N. *Why Survive? Being Old in America*. New York: Harper and Row, 1975.
This book provides a thoughtful overview of aging and the particular concerns encountered with growing old in the United States. Some of the specific data regarding Federal programs has changed, but the central issues have not.

Dayringer, R., ed. *Pastor and Patient: A Handbook for Clergy Who Visit the Sick*. New York: Jason Aronson, 1982.
Compared to *The Hospital Handbook* this resource provides more depth regarding ministry to patients with specific types of illnesses. As a companion book to *The Hospital Handbook*, it makes a complementary resource for the pastor's library. The authors of individual chapters are persons who are very capable caregivers and they write from the wealth of their personal skill and experience.

Jonsen, A.R. and Siegler, M. *Clinical Ethics*. New York: Macmillan Press, 1982.
If one book is to be selected in the field of medical ethics, this is the book to read. The authors present an excellent overview of the issues in such a way that the reader emerges with a good introduction to the field.

The Journal of Pastoral Care. Kutztown Publishing Company, P.O. Box 346, Rt. 222 and Sharadin Rd., Kutztown, Pennsylvania 19530.
This journal addresses a variety of practical and theological concerns in the delivery of pastoral care and counseling. A subscription provides four issues annually. Its contents should prove increasingly valuable to the ministry of the church.

Journal of Religion and Health, Human Sciences Press, 72 Fifth Avenue, New York 10011.
This journal publishes a variety of articles relevant to pastoral ministry. It is committed to a philosophy of the indivisibility of human well-being: physical, emotional, and spiritual.

Kirkly-Best, E., Kellner, K.R., et al. "On Stillbirth: An Open Letter to the Clergy." *The Journal of Pastoral Care* Vol. XXXVI(1), March 1982, pp. 17–20.
Suggestions are presented about how a minister, priest, or rabbi might be helpful in aiding parents through a stillbirth. The focus is on grief and aftercare as the most important areas of the functions of clergy. The authors represent the viewpoint of a physician, nurse, and social worker.

Knight, J.A. "The Minister as Healer, the Healer as Minister." *Journal of Religion and Health* Vol. 21(2), Summer 1982, pp. 100–114.

The author provides a sophisticated and sensitive discussion of the work of the pastor as a healer and the special opportunities this role provides. The priesthood of all believers is incorporated in the healer as minister, and similarities between ancient and modern healing are highlighted.

Meserve, H.C. "Guidelines For Health." *Journal of Religion and Health.* Vol 18(3), 1979, pp. 171–175.

This editorial provides a well-written, succinct, persuasive argument for taking personal responsibility for one's own health status. It provides three separate sets of guidelines as action plans which could be utilized by an individual or a group. For a church wanting to discuss issues of preventive health care few single articles would be more useful.

Oates, W.E. *The Christian Pastor.* Philadelphia: The Westminster Press, third edition, 1982.

This book has become a classic in learning the work of the pastor. Although it has been in print for twenty years, it remains a very useful resource. Every minister should have read it once, and a periodic review will be a source of renewal.

Oates, W.E. *Confessions of a Workaholic.* Nashville: Abingdon Press, 1978 (1971).

A very helpful book in examining work style. Dr. Oates speaks to persons in general who are overworked as a preferred style. The pastor can use this material to assess orientation to work, reevaluating time available for family and self.

Oates, W.E. and Lester, A. *Pastoral Care in Critical Human Situations.* Valley Forge, Pa.: The Judson Press, 1969.

Along with Dayringer's book, this earlier work provides another helpful resource in understanding specific pastoral issues in caring for persons experiencing major life crises. The authors utilize several resource persons who have specialized in areas such as mental retardation, chronic illness, and childbirth.

Robertson, J.A. *The Rights of the Critically Ill.* Cambridge, Ma.: Ballinger Publishing Company, 1983.

This book provides a helpful discussion of current legal rights as they relate to the doctor, family, and patient making decisions about dying and critically ill patients. The organization of the book makes it highly readable. The author poses a straightforward question and then discusses each answer. The questions are organized in such a way to address larger topics, such as "the rights of critically ill children."

Wagner, J.T. "A Leaderless Approach to a Minister's Peer Support Group."*Journal of Religion and Health* Vol. 21(3), Fall 1982, pp. 228–234.

A support group for ministers is described which is applicable to any community. The example group met for over ten years. Such a group can be used for continuing education purposes, including sharing case material related to the crisis of illness and providing pastoral care to parishioners.

Wanzer, S.H., Adelstein, S.J., and Cranford, R.E., et al. "The Physician's Responsibility Toward Hopelessly Ill Patients." *The New England Journal of Medicine* Vol. 310(15), April 12, 1984, pp. 955–959.

This brief, but comprehensive article carefully addresses the professional issues facing the physician in caring for a hopelessly ill patient. It is an attempt to put forward a set of guidelines which could become standards for practice. Ministers should be familiar with this thoughtful discussion.

Resources for Prayer, Scripture and Sacrament | 4

Most clergy agree that prayer is a necessary and appropriate part of the pastoral visit. At that point consensus ends. We range from the high church person who reflexively reaches for the prayer book when asked to pray to the free church person who believes any preparation betrays the inspiration of the Spirit. With these two points of the continuum as brackets I offer some guidelines and resources both for prayer and scripture, including a word on the integration of prayer and current trends in wholistic health.

Let us begin with a basic theological foundation of prayer. We affirm first that God is present with us always, seeking healing for us. Secondly, God does not send illness as punishment. Even though all of us know this, it is easy for a person who is ill to revert to superstitious religion which suggests that this particular affliction may be willed by God. We participate in a world of nature set free which has all kinds of capacity to become destructive. But God does not equal nature. John A.T. Robinson says that God does not cause the cancer, but God's face may be found in the cancer. This means that God is ever present, always with us, always accessible, always struggling in us and with us for healing. Our pain is God's pain, as God suffers with us.[1]

---

1. John A.T. Robinson, *Explorations Into God*, Stanford, CA: Stanford University Press, 1967, pp. 116–18.

God is also with us in a very personal way. The prayers by the bedside are good times to focus on the image of God incarnate, personally present in Jesus Christ, and thus alive in human form. God is divine energy within us. God is not deaf or distant, in need of being implored to be close to us. God is as close to us as the air we breathe and the heart that beats within us. God is in the healing blood which flows through our veins, but God is not limited to bodily systems.

Our stance before God, then, is one in which we envision ourselves becoming open to the light and power of God's love. The images of prayer are of open hands rather than of a clenched fist, of facial muscles relaxing rather than a furrowed brow, of deep and restful breathing rather than the gasps of intense supplication. Prayer need not be a stressful search for God but a nurturing acceptance of God's inexhaustible love. To pray this way is to begin to heal.

In fact it is sometimes worth understanding that the sick and hurting parts of our body are loved by God, unconditionally just as we are all loved by God, unconditionally.

Flora Wuellner of Pacific School of Religion says that prayer is divine energy received and released. She offers an image of this energy as light, and many parts of our lives put up blocks to the reception of this light. Prayer is meant to rearrange and move these blocks away to let the light shine into our lives. What the world calls a miracle, she says, is when all the blocks are gone and the light streams in. It is important to pray for the whole person to receive this light rather than to pray for specific symptoms. "Don't worry about end results—release the person or situation into God's healing love."[2]

Such a position releases one from the old dilemma of whether or not to pray for healing. I have been in that bind where to pray for a specific healing seemed manipulative and selfish yet the formula "not my will but thine be done" unintentionally suggested that God's will might be something other than healing.

In the context of prayer suggested by Flora Wuellner, I am much more comfortable in praying that a person may be opened to that healing power of God. Thus I turn the results over to God rather than struggle with the specific nature of healing.

Each of us has a different sense of just how healing occurs. We carry our own various forms of resistance of healing as well as our different affirmations of the place of God in the healing

---

2. Flora Wuellner, "Prayer, Fatigue and Spiritual Burnout," a Workshop at Pacific School of Religion, July, 1982.

process. Rather than debate those specific points, I believe it is important to pay attention to how the resistance and affirmation of healing function in our own lives and listen to clues of how they are operating in the life and illness of the patient before us. There is a mystery in prayer beyond which none of us can ever fully penetrate.

Remember, you are one of many healers. It is not up to you to be perfect. It is only up to you to be a channel for God's healing love to flow through you to the person before you in need. Prayer has a way of opening a door for God's love to flow through us.

Here are four elements for prayer. First, be aware of your own theology of prayer, the traditions, hopes, fears, and joys of your prayer life.

Second, with this background in mind, listen with care to the patient throughout your visit. Hear her hopes and fears, and remember them when it comes time to pray.

When you are with a patient who is chronically ill, hospitalized for a long period, you may have spent time in your visit hearing precious stories of childhood, falling in love, child raising, careers. Lift up these memories in prayer for their strength and power.

Third, touch the person when you pray. Hold his hand or gently touch his arm or forehead. The touching of a person symbolizes God's love holding the whole person, body and spirit.

Fourth, include in prayer a reminder that many people—church, family, and friends—are remembering this person in prayer and let the patient feel surrounded by this love as well.

These are suggestions, guidelines which make all prayer opportunities for healing and renewal.

This is a good place to look at wholistic health and meditation. Much is being written and shared about the role each of us plays in our own health and well-being. We are beginning to understand how our emotions contribute to our physical condition. The good news about this is that if we can begin to take some responsibility for our own illness, we have that much more power in participating in our own recovery. The bad news is that the last thing the seriously ill person needs is any suggestion that this illness is in some way his own fault. Therefore, we need to be careful with the language of personal responsibility and health.

It is good to become familiar with the better resources in wholistic health. Norman Cousins gives an excellent account of one man's struggle through serious illness through significant self-awareness.[3] Cousins believes that laughter is an important part of anyone's recovery. It is jogging for the soul. Cousins imported his own Marx Brothers movies into his room until he made such noise with his laughter that the hospital discharged him early.

Carl and Stephanie Simonton offer one of the finest guides for patient or pastor in understanding the individual's role in healing.[4] Dennis and Matthew Linn offer a thorough exploration of forgiveness and healing memories.[5]

Each of these resources encourages the patients to explore their own role in healing and at the same time cautions against second-guessing the physicians and becoming diagnosticians themselves.

You may want to incorporate into your prayers some of the methods used in meditation, or "depth prayer." Again, it is important to be sensitive to the needs and traditions of the patient and your own comfort with this style of prayer. Here is a general outline of the elements of meditation which can sometimes be combined with traditional bedside prayer.

As you prepare for prayer ask the patient to begin by breathing deeply and comfortably. You may even suggest the visualization of that deep breathing as inhaling the spirit of God.

Ask the patient to focus piece by piece on every part of the body, beginning with the forehead, flowing down to the neck, shoulders, arms, hand, upper and lower back, buttocks, thighs, calves, and feet, relaxing each part of the body.

Sometimes it may be appropriate to ask the patient to go back now and focus on any part of the body that is tense or hurting. Let her send the love of God to that hurting place, a love which accepts and surrounds every part of us unconditionally, just as God loves every one of us unconditionally. Let the love flow to that hurting place for a moment.

You may ask the patient to picture himself in a place of special joy and beauty, either real or imagined. This may be a remembered scene in the mountains or at the seashore. It may be an imaginary room or a room at home. It can just be a beautiful meadow in a park full of sunshine. Let the patient take a few minutes to focus on such a place of personal peace and power.

---

3. Norman Cousins, *op. cit.*

4. Carl and Stephanie Simonton, *Getting Well Again*, New York: Bantam Books, 1978.

5. Dennis and Matthew Linn, *Healing Life's Hurts*, Paramus, NJ: Paulist Press, 1977.

Now let the patient concentrate on her particular illness. Simonton says to picture it in any way that makes sense.[6] Ask the patient to visualize it in such a way that he can see the malfunction. Then picture too the body's healing forces overcoming that illness. Picture any medication working to destroy the sickness and empower the tissues of life. Visualize that hurting part well again and functioning as part of the body. Then ask the patient to see himself well again resuming his normal functions. Let the patient feel the healing power of God in whatever way makes sense to him.

Then slowly return your focus to his time and place, closing perhaps with silence and traditional words of prayer. Find out how the patient felt about the exercise. If the patient thought this meaningful, then encourage the patient to continue and share this exercise again and again. Interpret it as a gift of God that is useful if it becomes part of the recuperation process.

It is also possible to incorporate elements of this type of meditation in the format of prayer you are traditionally comfortable with.

When using any new format, always ask the patient how she felt in that process and listen to the feedback for further prayers and meditations.

Sample prayers are included here as guidelines and starting points for hospital prayers at the bedside.

Prayers

(1)   A prayer of intercession.

O God, we open our hearts to you in this time of sickness, and time of confusion, a time full of both fear and hope, questions and thanksgiving.

We pray that N._____ may feel your healing power in this moment. May he (she) feel this power as close to him (her) as the air he (she) breathes, as the blood running through his (her) veins, as the hands that hold him (her) in this moment. May he (she) know that in moments such as this you, O God, suffer with us, and guide us, always working for the mending of what is broken.

---

6.   Simonton, *op. cit.* pp. 75–80.

We pray that N._____ may feel the love of family and friends who remember him (her) in prayer, that N._____ may feel this love as a warm comforting light holding him (her) in the gentleness of grace.

O God, you are a tender shepherd who leads us through dark valleys to places of light and peace. Guide and keep us now that we might not lose sight of your love. Amen.

(2)   *A prayer when stories and memories have been shared.*

O God, we have shared a special time together this day. In the midst of sickness and pain, hearts have been opened, stories of life told, hopes risked, sorrow named.

We thank you for the good stories of N._____'s life. Surround these stories in grace that they may be a golden link with precious life, sustaining him (her) in the difficult times, and carrying him (her) to times of joy and light.

We thank you for the grace of lives shared, that in the telling of stories there is the communion of hearts and the bonding of friends.

And with the strength of this moment, we pray for continued strength, for stories yet untold, and experiences of life yet unmet. Grant us faith and courage for such moments. Amen.

(3)   *A prayer when the illness or surgery is minor, but still requiring hospitalization.*

O God, in times like this, when the normal routine of life is broken, we pray for a special sense of your presence. Though what N._____ faces does not carry great threat or deep danger, this is a moment of some fear and apprehension. We pray for calm and understanding, for the power of healing, and a vision of good recovery. Let N._____ use this time of rest for good purpose and then return to the tasks that lie ahead with new strength and care. Amen.

(4)   *A prayer for strength and hope.*

We pray to you, God, as the very heart of life, breaking, hurting, suffering with us. For how else would you understand our struggle if you did not hurt with us?

We pray that N._____ may see you as gentle

strength and seek to understand
how you are also the laughter which mends the brokenness,
the soothing peace after a long cry,
the vision of hope which appears after the tears wash away.

We pray that N.＿＿＿＿＿＿ may see you as one who
has chosen him/her. Give us all new life, new laughter, new
awareness of the beauty of life. Raise us up as images of
hope to the despairing, and bringers of softness to a world
hardened by pain.

O God, we pray to you as the very heart of life, beating
your rhythm of healing within us. Amen.

(5)   *A prayer in a time of confusion.*

O God, we are a mixture here indeed.
We hope, we doubt.
We rise, we fall.
We fidget, we fuss.

And then we experience a rising from some mysterious
place.
We hear you call our names.
We turn and listen in faith.

We pray now for N.＿＿＿＿＿＿ who in a difficult time
needs the calming touch of grace, the blessing of peace.

We pray for N.＿＿＿＿＿＿ that (s)he may hear the word
you have for her/him in this moment. Amen.

(6)   *A prayer in a time of fear and anxiety.*

There are times, O God, when it seems that the chain
of life which held us together is broken, and we feel ourselves
hurtling through a place of darkness and despair.

In this moment we pray for your everlasting arms to catch
and hold us, for angels to send help in the night, for light to
break the darkness and grant us comfort and rest.

Open our eyes that we may see such visions,
Open our hearts that we may receive such love.

Relax our tightened bodies that we may find the comfort
of the everlasting arms.

We pray especially for N.＿＿＿＿＿＿ that (s)he may feel
that chain of life connected again, linking friends and families,
faith and future, hope and love in a golden circle.

Give us all grace in times of need, to give and receive your
love which flows like an everlasting stream. Amen.

(7)   A prayer in a time of difficult change.

O God, there are days when we wake and discover that the landscape has changed.
We suddenly notice that the light suggests a later season,
      The land is different,
Growth has changed some people and removed others.
There are days like this when we feel alone, with no path to follow.
In these days, O God, you push us deep into the river of faith.
And there we find you flowing with the ever changing stream of our lives.
We sense your pulse in the beating of our hearts.
We hear your spirit in the rhythm of our breath.
We feel your grace in the cleansing wash of tears.
We experience your release in the burst of laughter.
And we find that what we feared was lost.
In all those changes is ourselves,
and we are found.
We pray, O God, for N.＿＿＿＿＿ in this time of change, for the discoveries that through the landscape changes, the land is still the same. May N.＿＿＿＿＿ find you in a lonely time as you open the deep gifts of his (her) life to him (her). Amen.

(8)   A prayer in a time of sudden reversal or crisis.

Sometimes, God, we make it through life just fine.
And we thank you for those moments,
that strength.
But this is not that time.
This seems to be a time when none of that works,
When our lips dry up, our voices fail, and strength to get back up
doesn't seem to be there.
In this moment we turn to you,
Praying especially for N.＿＿＿＿＿,
That (s)he feel the power of resurrection faith.
That (s)he understand that no matter how much our lives may falter,
Nothing passes away, nothing is lost,
and all is touched with the newness of life in your spirit.
We pray for N.＿＿＿＿＿, in need of a morning light to overcome the shadow that now looms.

Surround N.＿＿＿＿＿ with your light in the renewal
of life,
the healing of wounds, and the prevailing power of love.
Amen.

(9) *A prayer in a time when a special hope is needed or has been
shared.*

O God, there are moments like this when you catch us
unaware. For in this room it seems that we may be drained of
all spirit, and suffered all we can bear, then, deeper than our
hurt, the rising seed of faith catches us unaware.
We pray that N.＿＿＿＿＿ may feel this rising silently
like the dawn,
like the sigh of a child when he cannot cry any longer
and he puts his head on our shoulder in rest,
like the first seed that rises from the garden's earth,
like a hand slipping into ours to hold.
O God, we thank you for moments such as this, when
you catch us unaware. May N.＿＿＿＿＿ continue to
experience your gentle rising within him (her). Amen.

(10) *A prayer to be shared in conjunction with Psalm 23.*

O God you are a tender shepherd.
You lead us through dark valleys to
places of quiet and rest.
In this moment we pray for N.＿＿＿＿＿
that (s)he may feel your guidance through this time of
    struggle,
that (s)he may see the light of your love ahead
and feel the touch of your hand gently leading. Amen.

(11) *A prayer to be offered in times of sharing hopes, wishes, and
dreams when a good vision of the future is appropriate.*

We pray for good wishes Lord,
for finding people to love and love us,
for doing work that matters,
for uncovering the key to truth,
and finding meaning in the door it unlocks.
We pray for beautiful mountains to climb
and gentle seashores to walk.
We pray for dream houses of peace,
and families to enjoy each other in love.

We pray for healthy bodies,
and the renewed energy to live our dreams.
We pray for our church that it may bring us truth on the
    wings of wishes,
and wishes on the clouds of truth.
We ask, seek, and knock.
Let us see you opening a door within us,
a sleeping friend,
a gentle parent,
just waiting to be asked.
Amen.

(12)   *A prayer/guided meditation of trust.*

Gently relax yourself, breathing deeply, releasing tension,
sending God's love to the hurting places in your body.
See in your heart the prayer of the lilies of the field and the
birds of the air.
See yourself soaring above your worries like a bird.
Feel God's love taking care of you as you look down and
see your worries lying far below you on the ground.
Ask what could those worries offer you?
Would they make you stronger?
Could they make you live longer?
Soar like a bird over your worries as they drift away.
Shift your image to the wild flowers.
See yourself clothed in the beauty of the wild flowers, blowing
in the wind.
Trust the beauty which grows in you from God.
Without your worries, clothed in beauty, listen to God in your
heart...
Pray for eyes to see God's kingdom within you and surround-
ing you. Amen.

(13)   *A prayer for angels, messengers of God when it seems too
hard to even reach for God.*

O God, open our eyes to angels,
when you seem too far away to even call for help,
angels who hold our hands in dark nights of pain,
angels who show us a well of cool water when we feel so
parched we fear we will not make it,
angels of healing,
tender healers who mend our broken bodies,
loving healers who comfort our broken hearts,

wounded healers who take our pain upon themselves.
Rekindle our sense of wonder God, that we may name,
nurture, and call forth our angels as they nurture us.
Open the wonder of our faith, that in these quiet moments
we may hear, even faintly, the beating of angel wings.
Amen.

These are free prayers, designed to fit different moods
and situations. Let them suggest images to you, then use whatever
symbols, images, phrases, or ideas that open you to a spirit of
healing and grace.

Another powerful way to share the presence of God
with patients is in the reading of scripture. Neither prayers nor
scripture should be a substitute for listening and sharing the concerns
of the patient. Instead, they are ways to bring comfort and strength,
a reminder that none of us is alone, whether as visitor or patient.

Often the scripture lesson of the Sunday past is good
to share. This is a way to connect the patient with the life of the
congregation, and you may share your thoughts as they related to
that passage.

Listed below are other scripture passages which meet a
variety of needs for the hospital patient. These passages often suggest images for a closing prayer. Different translations often shed
new perspectives on traditional readings. In some cases more than
one version is offered, just to demonstrate the various directions the
same passage can take. Above all, be sensitive to the needs of the
patient for the familiar or the new.

Scripture References

Psalm 23 (RSV)

The LORD is my shepherd, I shall not want;
  he makes me lie down in green pastures.
He leads me beside still waters;
  he restores my soul.
He leads me in paths of righteousness
  for his name's sake.
Even though I walk through the valley of the shadow of
    death,
  I fear no evil;
for thou art with me;
  thy rod and thy staff,

> they comfort me.
> Thou preparest a table before me
>   in the presence of my enemies;
> thou anointest my head with oil,
>   my cup overflows.
> Surely goodness and mercy shall follow me
>   all the days of my life;
> and I shall dwell in the house of the LORD
>   for ever.

Psalm 23 *(Psalms Now)*

> The LORD is my constant companion.
> There is no need that He cannot fulfill.
> Whether His course for me points
>   to the mountaintops of glorious ecstasy
>   or to the valleys of human suffering,
>   He is by my side,
>   He is ever present with me.
> He is close beside me
>   when I tread the dark streets of danger,
>   and even when I flirt with death itself,
>   He will not leave me.
> When pain is severe,
>   He is near to comfort.
> When the burden is heavy,
>   He is there to lean upon.
> When depression darkens my soul,
>   He touches me with eternal joy.
> When I feel empty and alone,
>   He fills the aching vacuum with His power.
> My security is in his promise
>   to be near to me always,
>   and in the knowledge
>   that he will never let me go.

Psalm 36:7-9

> (RSV as adapted in the *Inclusive Language Lectionary*, Year
> C, National Council of Churches, Pilgrim Press, 1985 p. 53.)
> How precious is your steadfast love, O God!
>   All people may take refuge in the shadow of your wings.
> They feast on the abundance of your house,
>   and you give them drink from the river of your delights.
> For within you is the fountain of life;
>   in your light do we see light.

Psalm 46 (RSV)

God is our refuge and strength,
a very present help in trouble.
Therefore we will not fear though the earth should change,
though the mountains shake in the heart of the sea;
though its waters roar and foam, though the mountains tremble
with its tumult.
There is a river whose streams make glad the city of God,
the holy habitation of the Most High.
God is in the midst of her, she shall not be moved;
God will help her right early.
The nations rage, the kingdoms totter;
he utters his voice, the earth melts.
The LORD of hosts is with us; the God of Jacob is our refuge.
Come, behold the works of the LORD,
how he has wrought desolations in the earth.
He makes wars cease to the end of the earth;
he breaks the bow, and shatters the spear,
he burns the chariots with fire!
"Be still, and know that I am God.
I am exalted among the nations,
I am exalted in the earth!"
The LORD of hosts is with us;
the God of Jacob is our refuge.

Psalm 90:1-1 (RSV)

LORD, thou hast been our dwelling place in all generations.
Before the mountains were brought forth,
or ever thou hadst formed the earth and the world,
from everlasting to everlasting
thou art God.

Psalm 91:1-4 (TEV)

Whoever goes to the LORD for safety,
whoever remains under the protection of the Almighty,
can say to him,
"You are my defender and protector.
You are my God; in you I trust."
He will keep you safe from all hidden dangers
and from all deadly diseases.
He will cover you with his wings;
you will be safe in his care;
his faithfulness will protect and defend you.

Psalm 103 (RSV) 1-17

Bless the LORD, O my soul;
  and all that is within me, bless his holy name!
Bless the LORD, O my soul,
  and forget not all his benefits,
who forgives all your iniquity,
  who heals all your diseases,
who redeems your life from the Pit,
  who crowns you with steadfast love and mercy,
who satisfies you with good as long as you live
  so that your youth is renewed like the eagle's.
The LORD works vindication
  and justice for all who are oppressed.
He made known his ways to Moses,
  his acts to the people of Israel.
The LORD is merciful and gracious,
  slow to anger and abounding in steadfast love.
He will not always chide,
  nor will he keep his anger for ever.
He does not deal with us according to our sins,
  nor requite us according to our iniquities.
For as the heavens are high above the earth,
  so great is his steadfast love toward those who fear him;
as far as the east is from the west,
  so far does he remove our transgressions from us.
As a father pities his children,
  so the LORD pities those who fear him.
For he knows our frame;
  he remembers that we are dust.
As for (hu)man(kind), (their)his days are like grass;
  (t)he(y) flourish(es) like a flower of the field;
for the wind passes over it, and it is gone,
  and its place knows it no more.
But the steadfast love of the LORD is from everlasting to
    everlasting
  Upon those who fear him,
  and his righteousness to children's children.

Psalm 121

I lift up my eyes to the hills.
  From whence does my help come?
My help comes from the LORD,
  who made heaven and earth.

He will not let your foot be moved,
  he who keeps you will not slumber.
Behold, he who keeps Israel
  will neither slumber nor sleep.
The LORD is your keeper;
  the LORD is your shade
  on your right hand.
The sun shall not smite you by day,
  nor the moon by night.
The LORD will keep you from all evil;
  he will keep your life.
The LORD will keep
  your going out and your coming in
  from this time forth and for evermore.

Psalm 121 (TEV)

I look to the mountains;
  where will my help come from?
My help will come from the LORD,
  who made heaven and earth.
He will not let you fall;
  your protector is always awake.
The protector of Israel
  never dozes or sleeps.
The LORD will guard you;
  he is by your side to protect you.
The sun will not hurt you during the day,
  nor the moon during the night.
The LORD will protect you from all danger;
  he will keep you safe.
He will protect you as you come and go
  now and forever.

Psalm 121 *(Psalms Now)*

Where should I look for help in my need?
To majestic mountain peaks that probe our skies
  or to giants of industry that hem in our cities?
To satellites that circle our world or to computers that
  store up our knowledge?
The answer to my problems
  and the fulfillment of my needs
  must come from God Himself,
  from Him who created skies and mountains

and (hu)man(ity) to dwell in their midst.
He is a great God who knows our every desire.
  whose watchful eye is upon us night and day.
We can make no move without His knowledge.
His concern for his children is constant;
  His love for them is eternal.
And thus the LORD will keep you,
Shielding you from the forces of evil
  as a shade tree shields you
  from the rays of the blazing sun.
He does care for you,
  and He will fight with you
  against the enemies of your soul.
Whether you be coming or going,
  He knows the course you take,
  and He will go before you.

Psalm 131:1-2 (RSV)

O LORD, my heart is not lifted up,
  my eyes are not raised too high;
I do not occupy myself with things too great and too marvelous
    for me.
But I have calmed and quieted my soul,
  like a child quieted at its mother's breast
  like a child that is quieted is my soul.

Psalm 139:1-18, 23-24 (NEB)

LORD, thou hast examined me and knowest me.
Thou knowest all, whether I sit down or rise up;
  thou hast discerned my thoughts from afar.
Thou hast traced my journey and my resting places,
  and art familiar with all my paths.
For there is not a word on my tongue
but thou, LORD, knowest them all.
Thou has kept close guard before me and behind
  and hast spread thy hand over me.
Such knowledge is beyond my understanding,
  so high that I cannot reach it.
Where can I escape from thy spirit?
  Where can I flee from thy presence?
If I climb up to heaven, thou art there;
if I make my bed in Sheol, again I find thee.
If I take my flight to the frontiers of the morning

or dwell at the limit of the western sea,
even there thy hand will meet me
  and thy right hand will hold me fast.
If I say, "Surely darkness will steal over me,
night will close around me',
darkness is no darkness for thee
  and night is luminous as day;
    to thee both dark and light are one.
Thou it was who didst fashion my inward parts;
thou didst knit me together in my mother's womb.
I will praise thee, for thou dost fill me with awe;
wonderful thou art, and wonderful thy works.
Thou knowest me through and through:
  my body is no mystery to thee,
how I was secretly kneaded into shape
  and patterned in the depths of the earth.
Thou didst see my limbs unformed in the womb,
  and in thy book they are all recorded;
  day by day they were fashioned,
    not one of them was late in growing.
How deep I find thy thoughts, O God,
  how inexhaustible their themes!
Can I count them? They outnumber the grains of sand;
to finish the count, my years must equal thine.
Examine me, O God, and know my thoughts;
  test me, and understand my misgivings.
Watch lest I follow any path that grieves thee;
  guide me in the ancient ways.

Isaiah 43:1b-2, 5a (RSV)

Fear not, for I have redeemed you; I have called you by
    name, you are mine.
When you pass through the waters I will be with you
  and through the rivers, they shall not overwhelm you;
when you walk through fire you shall not be burned
  and the flame shall not consume you.
Fear not, for I am with you.

Isaiah 40:28-31 (RSV)

Have you not known? Have you not heard?
The LORD is the everlasting God,
  the Creator of the ends of the earth.
He does not faint or grow weary,

his understanding is unsearchable.
He gives power to the faint,
    and to him who has no might he increases strength.
Even youths shall faint and be weary,
    and young men shall fall exhausted;
but they who wait for the LORD shall renew their
    strength,
    they shall mount up with wings like eagles,
they shall run and not be weary,
    they shall walk and not faint.

Deuteronomy 33:27 (RSV)

The eternal God is your dwelling place,
    and underneath are the everlasting arms.

Matthew 11:28-30 (TEV)

Come to me, all of you who are tired from carrying heavy loads, and I will give you rest. Take my yoke and put it on you, and learn from me, because I am gentle and humble in spirit; and you will find rest. For the yoke I will give you is easy, and the load I will put on you is light.

Matthew 9:20-22 (TEV)

A woman who had suffered from severe bleeding for twelve years came up behind Jesus and touched the edge of his cloak. She said to herself, "If I only touch his cloak, I will get well."

Jesus turned around and saw her, and said, "Courage, my daughter! Your faith has made you well." At that very moment the woman became well.

Matthew 22:34-40 (TEV)

When the Pharisees heard that Jesus had silenced the Sadducees, they came together, and one of them, a teacher of the Law, tried to trap him with a question. "Teacher," he asked, "which is the greatest commandment in the Law?"

Jesus answered, " 'Love the LORD your God with all your heart, with all your soul, and with all your mind.' This is the greatest and the most important commandment. The second most important commandment is like it: 'Love your neighbor as you love yourself.' The whole Law of Moses and the teaching of the prophets depend on these two commandments."

Mark 10:46-52 (TEV)

They came to Jericho, and as Jesus was leaving with his disciples and a large crowd, a blind beggar named Bartimaeus son of Timaeus was sitting by the road. When he heard that it was Jesus of Nazareth, he began to shout, "Jesus! Son of David! Have mercy on me!"

Many of the people scolded him and told him to be quiet. But he shouted even more loudly, "Son of David, have mercy on me!"

Jesus stopped and said, "Call him."

So they called the blind man. "Cheer up!" they said. "Get up, he is calling you."

So he threw off his cloak, jumped up, and came to Jesus. "What do you want me to do for you?" Jesus asked him. "Teacher," the blind man answered, "I want to see again." "Go," Jesus told him, "faith has made you well."

At once he was able to see and followed Jesus on the road.

Luke: 11 9-10 (TEV)

"And so I say to you: Ask, and you will receive; seek, and you will find; knock, and the door will be opened to you. For everyone who asks will receive, and he who seeks will find, and the door will be opened to anyone who knocks."

John 1:1-5 (RSV)

In the beginning was the Word,
and the Word was with God,
and the Word was God.
He was in the beginning with God;
all things were made through him,
and without him was not anything made that was made.
In him was life, and the life was the light of men(all people).
The light shines in the darkness,
and the darkness has not overcome it.

Romans 8:26 (RSV)

Likewise the Spirit helps us in our weakness; for we do not know how to pray as we ought, but the Spirit himself intercedes for us with sighs too deep for words.

Romans 8:31b, 37-39 (TEV)

If God is for us, who can be against us?
No, in all these things we have complete victory through

him who loved us! For I am certain that nothing can separate us from his love: neither death nor life, neither angels nor other heavenly rulers or powers, neither the present nor the future, neither the world above nor the world below—there is nothing in all creation that will ever be able to separate us from the love of God which is ours through Christ Jesus our LORD.

I Corinthians 13:4-7, 13 (NEB)

Love is patient; love is kind and envies no one. Love is never boastful, nor conceited, nor rude; never selfish, not quick to take offense. Love keeps no score of wrongs; does not gloat over other men's sins, but delights in the truth. There is nothing love cannot face; there is no limit to its faith, its hope, and its endurance.

In a word, there are three things that last for ever: faith, hope, and love; but the greatest of them all is love.

II Corinthians 4:7-9 (TEV)

Yet we who have this spiritual treasure are like common clay pots, in order to show that the supreme power belongs to God, not to us. We are often troubled, but not crushed; sometimes in doubt, but never in despair; there are many enemies, but we are never without a friend, and though badly hurt at times, we are not destroyed.

Beyond the sharing of prayers and scriptures, the sacraments offer opportunities for healing mediated through the elemental symbols of the faith. The sacraments link the patient with God and the community of faith. Yet it often feels cumbersome to administer the sacraments in a hospital room. We offer here a simple format for the sacrament of Holy Communion. We encourage you to use this as a model to which you may adapt your own specific traditions of communion. As this communion celebration has been designed for the hospital setting, so you may also wish to take other sacraments and appropriate worship experiences from your traditions for the hospital setting.

Some patients feel that the communion in a hospital is a suggestion of terminal illness, so it is important to determine the patient's wishes and discuss the spirit in which the sacrament is offered.

If the patient does wish to share communion, make sure there is no medical problem in his receiving the elements. Then find out if this is something he wishes to share with family or friends or if he prefers to receive it alone.

If the room is shared with another patient, ask the neighboring patient if he wishes to share in the sacrament. Explain your understanding of the openness of the sacrament and respect that patient's preference.

Notify the nurse's station what you will be doing and ask that you not be disturbed during this period of time.

The most important guideline in celebrating communion in the hospital is to keep the sharing simple. The elements themselves contain so much symbolism and power, that we may rely on them more than our words.

Use parts of your church's standard eucharistic service so that the patient will feel the link with her own church.

The following outline is offered as a suggestion for a simple sharing of communion at the bedside.

Communion

(You may use this invitation or a specific reading from scripture.)

Luke tells us that two disciples met a stranger on the road the Sunday after Jesus had been crucified. They walked and talked, sharing their memories of their friend Jesus.

As evening fell they asked the stranger to share a meal with them.

When the stranger was with them at the table he took the bread, said the blessing, broke it and handed it to them. Their eyes were opened and they recognized him as the risen Christ.

In company with all believers in every time and beyond time, we come to this table to know him in the breaking of bread.

On the night Jesus was betrayed, he sat down to dinner with his friends. He took the bread in his hands, gave thanks, and blessed it.

Let us give thanks in prayer:

O God, we thank you for this moment, for the gift of bread, our link with you and all people who share with us in the breaking of bread. Amen.

(Break the Bread)

He broke the bread and gave it to them saying:

"This is my body which is broken for you."

In this bread the broken is made whole. Bread shared invites everyone to come and rest. Take and eat.

After dinner Jesus took the cup of wine, gave thanks and passed it among them with the words:

"This cup is the new covenant in my blood, poured out for you."

Let us share this cup, passed hand to hand among us, that we may know God's peace.

Prayer

O God let us be for one another, like the bread you are for us—
Nourishment for our friends,
Hope for those who look to us for direction,
Promise beyond dreams for our enemies.
O God let us be for one another, like the cup of blessing you are for us—
Unexpected beauty where all was parched and dry.
Amen.

Blessing

You have heard God's word, shared God's bread and cup, and offered yourself in prayer.

May this be a sign to you, that God is near,
and you are God's chosen,
Nourished and loved by God,
Never forsaken,
A light around you,
A firm ground of your being,
A good future in hope.
Amen.

Bibliography

Note: Always consult the classic denominational worship books for prayer and scripture resources for the sick. Both the new revisions and the classics in collections such as *The Book of Common Prayer* of the Episcopal Church. *The Lutheran Book of Worship, The Services of the Church* of the United Church of Christ. *The Union Prayerbook for Jewish Worship*, and *The Worshipbook* of the Presbyterian Church,

Footnote: An excellent resource for informal liturgies such as this is *Home Celebrations*, Lawrence Moser, S.J., Newman Press, N.Y. 1970.

to name just a few, have many references for use in hospitals. Often consulting the prayerbook of a different tradition opens new insights into spiritual guidance in the hospital setting.

Colquhoun, Frank, ed. *Prayers for Every Occasion.* Wilton, Ct.: Morehouse-Barlow, 1974.

Here is an extensive collection of over 1,500 prayers from diverse sources grouped by topic including many resources for healing.

Hunt, Cecil, and Suter, John Wallace. *Uncommon Prayers.* Greenwich, Ct.: Seabury, Press, 1955.

This is a collection of prayers for a variety of situations from a breadth of resources from the ninth to the twentieth century.

Linn, Dennis and Matthew. *Healing Life's Hurts.* Paramus, N.J.: Paulist Press, 1977.

This book combines classical disciplines of prayer and confession with wholistic health methodology.

Moser, Lawrence E., S.J. *Home Celebrations.* New York, N.Y.: Newman Press, 1970. This collection, which grew out of the Catholic liturgical renewal movement is designed for use in the home around specific occasions. As such it is informal and easily adapted to hospital visits which call for prayer and sacrament. There are specific prayers to be offered during a time of illness, and there is an excellent format for the Institution of the Eucharist in a non-church setting.

Oosterhuis, Huub. *Your Word Is Near.* New York, N.Y.: Newman Press, 1968.

These prayers by a Dutch Catholic priest combine classical liturgy with conversational tone. Headings include specific prayers for the sick.

Quoist, Michel. *Prayers.* New York, N.Y.: Avon, 1975.

These are confessional, first person prayers offered in a conversational tone dealing with secular themes and the Way of the Cross.

Special Situations 5

The AIDS Patient   Ministry to the AIDS patient presents a unique challenge to the pastor and the church. This challenge arises out of the nature of the disease and the circumstances usually involved in acquiring the illness. Without a thoughtful and accurate approach to understanding AIDS, ignorance, fear and prejudice become motivating forces for response and an effective ministry is not possible. Prior to providing specific suggestions for pastoral intervention, it is necessary to share current information about AIDS which is available at the time of this writing.

Acquired Immune Deficiency Syndrome (AIDS) is a retro-virus which probably entered the United States in the late 1970s. It was first recognized in 1981 as a new pathogen. Scientists most frequently refer to the AIDS virus as Human Immunodeficiency Virus (HIV). This name stands for information denoting a virus that attacks specific white blood cells (T-Lymphocytes) in the human blood. The virus attacks a person's immune system and damages his/her ability to fight other diseases.[1] At this time, no cure exists for the disease or a way to manage it. The most publicized treatment modality, AZT, seems to enhance the immune system, specifically T-cells,

---

1. Koop, C.E. "Surgeon General's Report on Acquired Immune Deficiency Syndrome." *Journal of the American Medical Association*, Vol. 256, No. 20, November 28, 1986, p. 2784.

and seems to decrease morbidity to opportunistic infections. But it is very expensive and cumbersome to use due to monitoring requirements.

As of May 1987 in the United States, over 35,000 cases of AIDS have been diagnosed and more than 20,000 deaths have resulted, including 494 children. The Center for Disease Control estimates that 1.5 million Americans are now HIV positive and by the end of 1991 there will be 324,000 diagnosed AIDS cases in the United States. The disease is present on every continent except Antarctica, with perhaps as many as 10-15 million infected worldwide, making it truly pandemic in nature. With possible exceptions of hunger or nuclear holocaust, AIDS poses the greatest threat to public health in our lifetime.

AIDS is spread through intimate sexual contact or exposure to the blood of an infected person. After the virus enters the blood stream, it attacks the T-Lymphocyte cells. Antibodies are produced by the immune system in response to the infection. Human Immunodeficiency Virus (HIV) antibodies can be detected by an ELISA (enzyme-linked immunosorbent assays) test, which is confirmed by the Western Blot. Although a person may be infected with the AIDS virus, they may not test HIV positive for several weeks or months following infection. Even if an infected person tests HIV antibody negative, s/he can transmit the disease to others unless appropriate precautions are taken.

Persons who are HIV positive have been known to remain symptom free for as long as nine years.[2] It is not known if every person who becomes infected will go on to develop ARC (Aids related complex)[3] or the disease known as AIDS.[4] When AIDS is diagnosed, the person usually does not survive beyond two years.

By pure happenstance AIDS entered the United States through the homosexual or bisexual community and by intravenous drug abusers who shared needles. Approximately 90% of diagnosed cases are found in these two sub-cultures. Because of the geographic clustering of these groups, 75% of all AIDS cases are located in New York, San Francisco, Los Angeles, and Miami. Because considerable prejudice exists against these subgroups, the

---

2. Ibid.
3. Symptoms might include loss of appetite, weight loss, fever, night sweats, skin rashes, diarrhea, tiredness, lack of resistance to infection, swollen lymph nodes.
4. Symptoms are a persistent cough, fever, difficulty breathing, pneumonia, Kaposi's Sarcoma, opportunistic infections.

initial, emotional response from the general public was to ignore the problem since the virus seemed to pose no threat to heterosexuals. Some early voices in the religious community suggested that AIDS was "God's judgment on the lifestyle of sinners." The result has been inadequate funding on the national level for research, education, and treatment.

It is now well understood that AIDS is no respecter of persons, regardless of age, sex, race, creed, national origin, or status. The greatest spread of the disease in future years will be among the heterosexual community.[5] Cases have also been diagnosed among infants born to infected mothers, hemophiliacs or other recipients of blood products prior to screening of blood donations, prostitutes, and the rare few health care professionals who had a needlestick accident or were inadequately protected while caring for HIV positive patients.

Research has dispelled many myths surrounding AIDS and particularly the fear persons feel about the risk of becoming infected. It is known that casual, non-sexual contact with an individual, who is HIV positive or who has ARC or AIDS will not result in transmission of the virus.[6] Several studies have shown that family members living with an AIDS patient, including children, have not converted to HIV positive.[7,8] Exceptions to this have been spouses who were sexually active with their partner without using a condom or children born to infected mothers. The family members studied shared household items like razors and eating utensils, used the same bathroom facilities, and exchanged hugs and kisses.

Although the HIV virus has been found in saliva and tears, there is no evidence of spread from these sources.[9] Nor is there risk from eating in restaurants where the chef is HIV positive or using public restroom facilities. There are no known cases of AIDS caused by insects, such as mosquitos, or from other animals, like

---

5. Koop, op. cit., p. 2783.

6. Eickhoff, T.C., et. al. "A Hospitalwide Approach to AIDS." Infection Control, Vol. 5, No. 5, 1984, p. 243.

7. Fischl, M.A., et. al. "Evaluation of Heterosexual Partners, Children, and Household Contacts of Adults with AIDS." Journal of the American Medical Association, Vol. 257, No. 5, February 6, 1981, pp. 640–644.

8. Friedland, G.H., et. al. Lack of Transmission of HTLV-III/LAV Infection to Household Contacts of Patients with "AIDS or AIDS-Related Complex with Oral Candidiasis." The New England Journal of Medicine, Vol. 314, No. 6, February 6, 1986, pp. 344–349.

9. Fischl, op.cit., p. 640.

cats and dogs.[10] Routine contact with fellow employees or children in schools, day care, or foster care poses no risk of infection.

Prevention of the spread of AIDS is largely related to individuals being adequately educated about the routes of transmission, including young people. When appropriate guidelines are followed, no one, save infants born to infected mothers, is helpless against being infected. The safest behavior for persons who do not wish to risk infection is to not use illicit drugs and practice sexual monogamy or celibacy. In a pluralistic society where behaviors frequently vary from these ideals, persons who use illicit drugs should not share contaminated needles. Condoms should be used when having sex. The Center for Disease Control also recommends that health care workers protect themselves from exposure to blood and body fluids. With the current understanding of AIDS, the behaviors described above should be adequate to dramatically slow the spread of infection.

Currently, some are calling for more drastic actions, such as mandatory testing (of high risk populations, all hospital admissions, and for marriage license applications), exclusion of HIV positive individuals from the work place or public schools, and quarantine. Mandatory testing would represent an enormous expense with questionable returns. It would not be useful in detecting infected persons who do not yet test positive. It would probably have the effect of driving persons underground who know they are at risk for infection out of fear that society would be punitive. Exclusion from the workforce or public schools would accomplish nothing positive since no proof exists that casual contact spreads the disease. For the same reason, quarantine is illogical, with the possible exception of individuals who repeatedly demonstrate an inability to protect others from infection.

Perhaps it is now becoming more clear why ministry to the AIDS patient or HIV antibody positive person is a challenge for the pastor and church. With the exceptions of children born to infected mothers, recipients of infected blood transfusions, health care professionals converted through work, or unknowing spouses, individuals who are HIV positive have participated in behaviors not approved by the church. Put harshly, it can be said that many infected persons knowingly took risks and are responsible for the unfortunate consequences.

Extending this familiar relationship between behavior and consequences into a theological framework, particularly in

---

10. Koop *op.cit.*, p. 2787.

the case of AIDS, is not easily accomplished. What sin deserves a death sentence? The position that God is punishing a person for either lifestyle or a momentary lapse seems to create a theological oxymoron of a "loving God." Such claims exhibit a self-serving posture similar to that when the church used fear of pregnancy as an argument against pre-marital sex. As was true prior to the discovery of birth control pills, the church continues the need to be responsible with education and to address the more complex issues regarding the "meaning" of sexual relationships.

It will necessitate a great deal of maturity for a church to be inclusive. Irrational fears and prejudices will likely be only partially alleviated through education. Theological understanding of the church and its role in human brokenness will play an equal role. The sharpest focus of concern perhaps lies in the "sin-suffering" connection. Throughout history the advent of plagues has been predominantly explained by the church as punishment for sin. Lepers were quarantined not only to contain the illness but as an added punishment for sin and presumed sexual promiscuity. The English Prayer Book, written in 1661, implied that healthy people were bastards because they had not received the fatherly correction of illness. In 1721, Cotton Mather, a Puritan, had to leave Boston temporarily because his cure for smallpox was viewed as violating the will of God's punishment. The first obstetrician to use anesthesia, William Simpson, was excommunicated because of the belief that women should have pain in childbirth.

The nature of God-ness as exemplified in the life of Christ gives frequent witness to a very different posture. Rather than assuming a position of judgment and exclusion, Jesus is often described as meeting the experiences of human brokenness, guilt and shame, with compassion, forgiveness, and restoration of dignity. No more appropriate illustration exists than the woman caught in adultery. To that experience of harshness and alienation he brought the sobering confrontation of a previously unacknowledged commonality with the accused. The stones which might have been used to execute judgement became a foundation for the possibility of fellowship. The cold rejection of exclusion was potentially set aside for the discovery of a more enriching way to live together.

A more recent example of a model for relating to AIDS patients is the church's ministry to singles and/or divorced persons. Through these programs the church has not felt its values about marriage to be threatened. At the same time, the church has recognized the realities of divorce or the preference of some to be single. Despite a failed marriage or a single lifestyle, persons have been accepted and affirmed in their need for faith and fellowship. These persons no longer have to leave the church; nor should the person diagnosed HIV positive or suffering from AIDS.

What is the meaning of the AIDS pandemic? Ignorance and fear will result in an answer which repeats errors of the past. An affirmation of the church's true nature prescribes bringing fellowship and care to alienation and suffering, which is the experience of the AIDS patient and his/her family. The answer to the meaning question is not to explain "Why?" but is found in the response of the church.

There are many needs to which pastor and church can bring ministry. Confidentiality may be the first issue of concern for persons who test HIV positive, as well as their families. This will be especially true in a church where rejection and judgement are guides to response. For the pastor to be offered an opportunity to minister, s/he will have to demonstrate an ability to respect privacy. Most pastors are capable of guarding the secret hurts and concerns of parishioners. Divulging information that a person has AIDS will put that individual at great risk in the community, including the work or school setting.

Although secrecy is an issue in relation to the general public, the pastor must assist the person who has the AIDS virus to find courage and behave appropriately with spouses and other significant persons. Families have a right to know, be ministered to, and be educated about how to stay involved with their loved one without risking infection. Disclosure to family members is not easy. It can be fraught with guilt and shame, particularly when a spouse has already been exposed and is possibly infected.

For single persons, particularly homosexuals, the moral task to change behavior is heightened. Homosexuals are mentioned because it is not unusual for them to have numerous casual sexual partners. Heterosexual singles may have several sexual partners, also. For each, however, disclosure of being HIV positive would threaten a relationship. Under all circumstances, precautions must be taken, such as the use of condoms and avoidance of any behavior exposing another to infection. When a person has been exposed to infection, the only responsible decision is to inform him or her.

To a thoughtful person, disclosure to family and significant others, as well as preventive behavioral changes seem obvious. Aside from shame and guilt, there are other issues which may result in the patient being less than thoughtful. Persons diagnosed HIV positive often live as with a death sentence. Understandably, living with such a gloomy outlook can result in feelings of denial, depression, anger, and even suicidal or homicidal feelings. When these emotions become too intense, thoughtful behavior is not always the result. For this reason, the pastor should encourage, and when possible, facilitate referral to a therapist. In addition, even if continued in total privacy, the pastor should provide an ongoing ministry of support and concern.

The necessity to inform a person who has been exposed poses an ethical and potential legal dilemma for the pastor, especially when s/he remains the primary helping person. The patient/ parishioner acts responsibly when the exposed person is informed. If the HIV positive person refuses, however, then the pastor must make a decision whether or nor to break the confidentiality and inform known persons who are at risk. Pastors must legally break this rule of confidentiality when the client is believed to pose a homicidal risk to others. At the time of this writing several persons who have knowingly exposed others to the AIDS virus have been charged with attempt to murder. While these arrests currently mirror public fear more than case law, a situation is represented where the pastor may have exclusive knowledge of persons at serious risk from another. Consultation with a legal advisor, discussion with denominational policy makers, and perhaps peer-group sharing may assist in arriving at a reasonable guideline useful in shaping professional behavior.

In many ways, the AIDS patient must be viewed as living with an illness which has features that are both chronic and terminal. For years, perhaps, the HIV person lives with fear that symptoms associated with ARC or AIDS will develop. Any relevant symptom heightens this fear. Monitoring and preventive interventions from health care professionals, on an out-patient basis, is usually appropriate. If and when symptoms af ARC or AIDS do develop their interventions increase, perhaps including hospitalization for the first time.

As was mentioned earlier, AIDS affects the immune system. Consequently, when hospitalized, the visiting pastor may be asked to wear protective clothing. These isolation garments may consist of mask, gown, gloves, and shoe covers. The mask and gloves especially contribute to a feeling of depersonalization. The sensitive pastor may be tempted to do without these items in order to feel more in "contact" or in "touch" with the patient. It should be remembered that in this case isolation garments are for the protection of the pastor and the patient. The pastor can acknowledge the awkwardness of the garments, but interpret them as one way of caring for the patient. The eyes, tone of voice, words and mere presence are adequate to convey pastoral concern.

If the present treatment approaches to AIDS continue, with no cure and difficulty in managing symptoms, the pastor should take initiative to encourage hospital staff or any health professionals who are church members and involved in care of AIDS patients. Despite the growth of hospice programs and its wonderful philosophy of care, most hospital employees are discouraged when intervention efforts are so overwhelmingly frustrated. Ninety percent of current AIDS patients range in age between twenty to forty-nine. Their numbers are increasing as will feelings of burn-out among hospital employees. Despite careful precautions being taken in caring for AIDS patients, health care professionals also fear inadvertent exposures which might result in conversion to a positive HIV. This fear must be managed through their professional skills and values, but an expression of appreciation from a pastor will be regarded as special encouragement.

The pastor should find an excellent source of help from a local AIDS network. They are present in many communities, sometimes supported by funding, volunteers, or both. Resources which are available to victims will include the names of physicians who will accept an AIDS patient. Other needed services are usually available, such as support groups and personal assistance. For information regarding the nearest network, contact AIDS Crisisline, New York: 1-800-221-7044. Another source of information is Drug Treatment Information 1-800-662-HELP.

In conclusion, we need an ethical framework for ministry to the victims of AIDS which is rational, responsible, and loving. To be rational, we need to stay informed. New information on AIDS is coming forth daily. We have to do our homework, understanding what is before us and the AIDS victim. Otherwise we are easily drawn in to fear born of ignorance. Good information can go a long way in calming hysteria.

We need to act responsibly on the information we have. To be responsible, we need to act with appropriate safeguards in our ministry and encourage others to do the same. Love is the final antidote to fear. "Perfect love drives out all fear," says I John 4:18b. Right now the health care providers, the family, and the friends of AIDS victims minister to these victims with their loving presence. As clergy, we are drawn into this circle with this same resource.

Shortly before Jesus was crucified, according to the gospel of Matthew, 26:6-13, he entered the home of Simon the Leper. There a woman came to Jesus with a wonderful jar of perfume which she poured over him. Most of our discussions of this passage focus on the meaning of this woman's act. We forget where Jesus was, in the home of a leper. He entered that home without fanfare and with no mention of an intended healing. A beauty flowed in that room that night, symbolized in the fragrance of the perfume. By sitting down to eat with Simon the Leper, Jesus was performing the ministry of a loving presence.

The AIDS victim is treated by the church and society today much in the same way the leper was treated in Jesus' day. Feared, labelled as unclean, seen to be reaping the harvest of sin, the leper was also excluded from society. Like Jesus entering the house of Simon the Leper, a loving presence is crucial to healing.

The Child is a Patient
All the gifts and skills of ministry come to focus in the experience of a child seriously ill. Perhaps no other life event renders persons so vulnerable. Deep within us there is a primitive, if not profound notion that everyone should have a past. Any threats to the child's accruing a past become symbols of how unfair life can be and how injustice is woven throughout the fabric of creation. Parents and other adults experience threats to the child as a feeling of having lost their future, their immortality. Offering faith in God must be done in the face of these realities, not as a means to remove them. Having an adult faith means affirming life despite the world being harsh at times. Creation may be "good," but it is not perfect. In the child's illness there is a great challenge for pastor, patient, family, and the entire caring community to undergird one another with faith, hope, and love. When one can no longer believe or hope, then there must be love. In time, hope and faith will return. Love, however, must never be absent.

I believe the pastor can have a significant ministry to the hospitalized child, but most often this will take the form of providing assistance through the parents. They will feel helpless enough in having to rely upon health professionals to provide "care" when in fact they would like to possess some of the concrete skills contributing to living treatment. Every effort should be made to reinforce the parental role and to guide its enactment so that the child experiences benefit in their love and concern.

For example, an early issue to be addressed is "How much should the child be included in knowing the diagnosis?" Most pediatricians or other physicians who treat children believe that including the child-patient in the communication process is desirable, including knowing the diagnosis. Some instances would surely exist where the adult understands more than the child. The intent is to avoid structuring an environment where the child senses that a "secret" exists. That kind of climate undermines trust, creates a sense of foreboding in the child, and ultimately results in loneliness. The parents may need the pastor's wisdom in structuring this type of communication pattern.

In those situations where parents express the wish to withhold information from the child, the intent is positive. They simply want to do what any sensitive parent does and that is to protect their child. The larger question, however, is that of intimacy. How close can we be to one another? Will our relationship allow only for positive feelings? Sometimes parents behave as if this is the case. Arguments, disagreements, emotional displays take place out of the child's sight. Most of us have memories as a child of parents being in another portion of the house to "problem-solve," though we knew they were upset, either by hearing raised voices or by other non-verbal clues before or after the confrontation. We didn't necessarily know what was the item of upset, but it was no secret that upset existed.

On the other hand, it is too superficial for the pastor to simply encourage "crying in front of the child." Observers during natural catastrophes such as earthquakes have pointed out that a child did not sense the fear or danger involved until it was seen in the facial expressions of the parent. It is crucial when feelings are shared with a child for the parent to add an explanation. For example, the parent can say, "Mother was crying because I don't want you to be ill. It's okay to cry when we feel that way. It feels better to share it with one another, just like we do during happy times." This kind of expression involves the child in parental feelings, teaches the child that feelings are to be shared, and models healthy behavior patterns which give the child permission to share feelings of all kinds. In time, a skillful pastor can work to help parents understand this style of communication.

There are some predictable benchmarks when stress and upset are most intense and pastoral intervention of a necessity. The time of diagnosis has already been mentioned. On occasion, prognostic information is given simultaneously with diagnosis. Regardless, it is the rare patient or family who "hears" all of what has been said during this period. It usually requires many more opportunities for questions to be asked, answers digested, and more questions put to the physician before any clarity begins to emerge. The pastor can be understanding with this process, as must the physician, who may be asked the same questions on repeated visits. Mechanisms of shock and denial soften the blow until reality can be incorporated more fully.

In those types of illnesses where a "remission" or apparent absence of disease occurs, the stage is set for tremendous disappointment when the patient relapses. During remission, fantasies can grow that the original diagnosis was wrong or that a combination of treatment and prayer have resulted in a cure. Many parents have indicated that the relapse of their child's illness was more difficult emotionally than hearing the diagnosis. Another benchmark, in addition to diagnosis, prognosis, and relapse, is any crisis event such as surgery. Other critical times might be such developments as a cardiac or respiratory arrest, or any other life-threatening episode. In illnesses where life will be shortened, the terminal phases usually begin when meaningful efforts to manage the disease no longer exist. Each of these times represent issues which provide opportunities for pastoral assistance and presence.

Throughout the course of a child's chronic or life-threatening illness, the minister should stay in close touch with the parents. Just as there are a number of times when intervention is in response to a crisis, there are other issues which may be present that are capable of quietly eroding a marriage. Tending to them prior to their becoming critical can enrich the marriage. The notion that a crisis will strengthen family relationships is a myth. Hard work can produce this result. Otherwise, there are too many problems that fracture and separate people. Much of the remainder of this chapter discusses those concerns. One or both parents may feel guilty that the child is ill. Sometimes this guilt is existential in nature. At other times it may be related to something the parent has done for which they believe punishment is being given. I have heard parents explain an illness as resulting from having given the child too hard a spanking. In a primitive sort of way, having an explanation, even an incorrect one, is better than embracing the notion that creation has the character of being whimsical or capricious. Assuming personal guilt or ascribing blame to God are frequent parental responses. Each is defeating, as one results in self-alienation while the other results in alienation from God. In these circumstances the pastor can bring a faithful type of loving concern that behaviorally affirms both the parents' and God's love without necessarily using "God-talk." Forgiveness and acceptance can be communicated without the frequent use of theological language. Eventually a time will come when the pastor can assume a priestly role and offer forgiveness and acceptance through the rituals of faith.

Another possible issue is communication problems between father and mother. This concern can be serious, even in good marriages. It is made more difficult by the time and energy necessitated by providing care for the child-patient. Maintaining two home fronts between the residence and hospital leaves little energy for one another. Sometimes the pastor can visit the hospital with the intent of allowing both parents to go out for a meal. When you do this, it is helpful to bring a game you know the child-patient enjoys. This type of planning is best done by arranging a "date" with the child, so everyone can plan ahead.

When the child is the focus of the pastor's visit, remember these general guidelines. They apply to hospitalization, whether the illness is life-threatening or the result of appendicitis. Remember that children are not necessarily as comfortable with verbal communication as are adults. Yet you must deal directly with the child. One pastor had a group of retired men in the church who made wooden toys. Each time he visited a hospitalized child a wooden toy accompanied him. The toy became a point of focus around which a visit could occur. Playing a game has already been mentioned. Watching "Mr. Rogers" together on television is another shared activity. Limits must be respected, including keeping things on the child's level as well as not being active in such a way to jeopardize treatment.

At times the breakdown in communication is for other reasons. One parent can take an extremely hopeful position on the prognosis, refusing to acknowledge the seriousness of it, while the other parent attempts to be more realistic. Sparks can fly when they try to talk about the feelings each is having. At other times, there is a cessation in sexual sharing. Fatigue can contribute to this, but there are usually other reasons. Guilt contributes to a lack of interest. "How can I 'indulge' myself when my child is so ill?" Sometimes anger at God or self frustrates the partners sharing themselves with one another. Fear of pregnancy which might produce another ill child is an additional reason.

Another increasingly common stress is the result of dual career families. When the child is hospitalized, who is going to leave work and provide companionship? On occasions, it is not possible for either parents to be at the hospital during the daytime hours. This problem is complicated by the presence of other children at home who are equally needful of routine attention. Even when legitimate reasons exist for parents being unable to stay at the hospital, I have seen them made scapegoats, particularly the mother, as being uncaring and without love for the child-patient.

Traditionally, it has been common in marital dyads for the wife-mother to be present at the hospital more often than the husband-father. Aside from dual career concerns, there are other problems which can exist. The pastor should be alert to them. One that is quite common is that the wife becomes the primary communication link between the hospital and the father. Fathers can feel less integrated into the decision-making process as well as more emotionally distant from hospital staff. This promotes an artificial delineation of roles in which the mother is pictured as being on the front line of the child's battle against illness, while the father is emotionally removed in order to provide an income and manage the household. One father eloquently expressed how lonely he felt when he said, "Whenever anyone inquires about my son's illness, they always say 'How is your wife doing?' They never ask how I feel!" Don't forget to recognize the tender feelings which fathers have. A child's illness is a "teachable moment" and many parents, especially fathers, reorder priorities as a result. An example is the decision to preserve more energy for family life, putting less, perhaps, into a career.

Families where divorce has occurred also present special concerns. When the child is hospitalized, both parents usually wish to have some involvement. Where residual tensions continue to exist, the pastor can assist in coordinating the contact between child and parent. Usually this is accomplished through the parent having custody making clear what is preferred. The ultimate issues don't change, however, which is that the parents continue to serve the child's best interests. The fact that they have divorced, and perhaps remarried, doesn't change that goal. At times, of necessity, it is best that both parents not be at the hospital together. Old scars thought to be healed can become tender again.

Single parents also have special needs. A child's illness usually is more than an intact nuclear family feels capable of handling. The single parent, usually the mother, can become quickly overwhelmed. The pastor can enlist helpers from the church fellowship who can work wonders in providing assistance. These helpers do not have to be particularly skilled except in being good people who are interested in helping. If there is a caution to selecting these helpers, it must be that they be non-judgmental. All parents feel guilty when their child becomes ill. The single parent can be especially vulnerable to this crippling form of self-accusation. No discussion ever need occur as to why this child is ill. What is needed is the loving support of a caring fellowship.

The pastor should be equally alert to the siblings of the child-patient. Sometimes direct intervention is called for, and on other occasions reminding parents of this concern is sufficient. In the demanding tasks everyone faces, other children who are not the patient can be overlooked. At times this includes the routine kind of daily upsets and needs which are basic but may seem dwarfed next to the child-patient's illness. When the illness is chronic in nature, this can create a lot of jealousy and resentment between the patient and brothers/sisters. One parent of a cystic fibrosis child gave postural drainage therapy to each of her young children until they were old enough to understand that this was a treatment and not to be confused with giving more love to one child than another.

Usually the concerns of siblings are more routine or particularly pertinent to what transpires at the hospital. One young lady, upon visiting her older brother who was having brain surgery, saw that his head had been shaved prior to the operation. She innocently asked, "Are they going to cut his head off next?" It would have been easy for a parent or pastor to hear this comment as a cute joke and make light of it. Sensitivity required that the remark become an opportunity for this concerned sister to have a more positive understanding of what her brother was going to experience. In addition to her concern, she was also formulating images of what it might be like to be a patient in a hospital. Careful attention to her needs and understandings also shaped any future experiences she might have with illness.

In our culture, certain illnesses, particularly cancer, have a powerful taboo associated with them. In the case of children, this taboo extends to areas I had never considered prior to my career in Chaplaincy. Many parents have shared a particularly harsh dimension to this taboo which every pastor ought to understand. Apparently, many children with cancer find that during periods of remission former playmates no longer come around as usual. The fear has been communicated that somehow the illness might be contagious, and other parents do not permit contact previously enjoyed in friendships. This is a form of abandonment that is especially difficult, because it adds to the sense of failure and rejection that every patient feels, even when a child. When the pastor observes this happening, or even prior to its occurrence, special educational efforts need to be made, utilizing physicians and nurses, to assist in avoiding this well-intended, but cruel and harmful, behavior.

Parents, especially fathers, have also expressed a similar concern for themselves. They have often said that following the diagnosis of their child they no longer felt as involved socially in the plans of others, particularly friends. In this case, the reasons most often given were that friends felt the parents did not want to be "disturbed" or "bothered." At times, understanding was needed in declining an invitation. As a general rule, however, parents wanted to continue being included in the network of relationships which had developed over the years. Behind many of the explanations, many of the parents felt that friends did not know what to say about the child's illness and so they imagined that contact would be harmful. Put more simply, many people felt uneasy being around the parents and so they stayed away, using the explanation that they really intended to be sensitive by doing so. The sensitive pastor knows that when life brings hard times the people experiencing difficulty always feel insecure as a result. "What did I do to deserve this? What do people think of me now?" are common feelings, if not always verbalized. The teaching ministry of the church can help bring a light into this darkness of misunderstanding which leads to loneliness.

Many illnesses are chronic in nature, even some of those which will shorten life. One of the characteristics of chronic illness is that the family must incorporate its realities into the daily routine. This may mean that a significant portion of resources, both financial and otherwise, become committed to the maintenance of health. Practically, this can result in a family being unable to enjoy some of life's pleasures. At other times, it can feel like the center of existence has become illness and all that it threatens. This feeling has its hazards, also. Rarely does it happen that a child will be abandoned by parents. It is not uncommon, however, for a parent or a sibling occasionally to wish the child-patient would die. Even the fleeting thought can result in tremendous guilt feelings. Equally as common is the tendency of parents to feel sorry for the child-patient and to treat him or her in an unnatural or special way. More clearly, the parents may refuse to feel anger at the child, or provide discipline, and may attempt to indulge the child's every express wish. The result can become a spoiled child who doesn't really feel loved or one that is burdened with guilt because so much of the family resources have become focused in his or her direction. If these issues become apparent to hospital staff some effort will be made to deal with them. It may well be that the pastor is the first to see clearly what is happening and find it necessary to take initiative in resolving an unhappy adaptation to illness. Even if hospital staff recognized the concerns, it may be the pastor who assists the family in the day to day adjustments in behavior. Even though everyone may finally agree that it is best to treat the child as normally as possible, it can be very difficult at first to change old patterns. Even doing the right thing can initially cause feelings of discomfort and guilt.

At the beginning of this chapter I mentioned that few life experiences rendered persons so vulnerable. Let me be more specific. In the first place, there is a new lifestyle to learn in terms of maintaining home fronts between the hospital and the place you always thought of as home. Second, there is the risk of illness becoming the pivotal consideration in every family decision. It needs to be pointed out as well that the pressures on the family may not result in deliberately abandoning the child but it can create a rupture in relationships such that divorce occurs. In families where a child dies, the divorce rate is significantly higher than what has already become an all too common phenomenon. In one study of families with a child seriously ill, it was discovered that eighty-eight percent experienced serious damage to effective family functioning and that there were multiple problems among survivors.[11] Of these problems, approximately eighty percent were described as developing only after the diagnosis of a child's serious illness.

Even if divorce does not occur, marital discord is far too common. Sibling problems may manifest themselves in changes in school behavior or in poor relations with the parents. This is particularly true when the siblings feel the parents withhold the truth as to the seriousness of the illness. Health problems can also increase among survivors. Sometimes these concerns are of a psychosomatic nature, such as colitis, ulcers, or hypertension. At other times, they may be psychological and involve substance abuse or require psychiatric intervention. Other emotional maladjustments can be functional in nature, such as the inability to fulfill a routine role activity, for instance, going to work or keeping house.

These points form a clear directive to the sensitive pastor. Attention to all family members during a child's serious illness represents a primary responsibility. And, this caring concern must extend far beyond a child's death, should that be the outcome. It may certainly be the case that the help a family requires is beyond the skill level or the hours a pastor has available. Referral to other professionals is appropriate at that time, but can be done in such a way that pastoral concern, as well as that of the church, continues to be felt by the family. No amount of theological sophistication can make pleasant such a life experience. Love, however, can transform all the pain and hurt into a bearable load such that life can be good again, in time.

Terminal
Illness
Loss of life, either resulting from a sudden, unexpected event or from prolonged illness will be a part of every minister's pastoral experience. Since 1970, few areas have received more attention in the literature and general media than has thanatology. Hospitals have become more aware of the special needs of patients and families experiencing life-threatening illness. Ministers have always had a unique place in death events as the rituals of faith and their enactment supply a clear pastoral role. The pastoral care of these persons and the subtleties involved are

11. Kaplan, D.M. and Smith, A., et al. "Family Mediation of Stress." *Social Work.* July 1973, pp. 60–69.

more difficult to grasp. It reminds me of the new graduate serving his first church who called a seminary professor for assistance following the death of a parishioner. "What do I do?" he asked. "Look over your notes and remember what we discussed in class," said the teacher. "We covered everything you need to know." The young pastor replied, "But you don't understand, this guy is really dead!"

The responsibility to be a good pastor during loss events is really yours. Perhaps several perspectives can provide a framework in shaping your ministry. First, with some exceptions, many illnesses which will shorten life are chronic in nature and extend over a period of several years. This means that much important work can be done prior to the death. Second, bereavement, or "grief work," is a process of adjustment which has both acute and chronic phases, often lasting several years or longer beyond the patient's death. Consequently, pastoral work begins at the point of diagnosis and is not completed until a reasonable adjustment to the loss has been achieved, usually several years later. Obviously, then, the notion of fulfilling the pastoral role through the funeral rituals is superficial, at best.

Another perspective is that living with and through serious illness is like running an ultra-marathon. It requires thoughtful planning, patience, endurance, and timely support. Although no one wants to experience it, this type of crisis has the potential of enriching relationships and of being a way into a more meaningful life. No pastor should use these phrases in an effort to reassure, lest they become cliches. It is enough to trust that the potential for goodness resides in what we would all agree is a life event no one would choose to experience.

A fourth perspective is that few persons are prepared to live with serious illness or face losing a cherished other. Our culture highlights youth, vitality, and health. It cloisters painful events. Most people receive medical treatment and die away from home. As a result, even though everyone experiences death, preparation is rarely part of normal developmental experience. It is helpful, therefore, for patient and family to have guides, teachers, or counselors to facilitate their way through what amounts to a "foreign country." Health care professionals will naturally have opportunities for intervention due to the role of the hospital. The largest time periods, however, will be those in the home community where the pastor is a primary resource.

Another aspect of awareness for the pastor is the possibility of significant bio-ethical issues in decision-making. In the case of terminal illness, modern medicine has the ability to sustain life beyond what is meaningful existence. Decisions to withhold or withdraw life-sustaining treatment require careful thought. If the pa-

tient is comatose, it is usually the family which must decide. In some
states, "natural death" acts recognize express wishes of the patient
in some form of the "Living Will," even after he or she becomes comatose. But the specifics of the law must be observed, and they vary
between states having such laws. Theological and ethical positions
must be carefully considered by the pastor *prior* to being in a
decision-making mode. They must include the ability to support
families while minimizing feelings of guilt. A President's
Commission[12] has produced a series of publications which can adequately inform regarding bioethical issues.

An additional perspective for the pastor to keep in mind
is the ultimate goal in the resolution of loss. It is that survivors are
able emotionally to "give up" the deceased, learn to live without
that person's presence, and be able to reinvest themselves in new
relationships as well as in life. This statement sounds so simple.
Between the time of diagnosis and the time that the survivor has
a glimpse that such an affirmation might be possible lies what might
well be the most difficult, painful, confusing life experience to come
his or her way. The time frame may extend over several years, during which the person lives with real uncertainty about ever being
able to make that affirmation.

In a primary way, the survivor has learned that a part
of living involves losing those persons who are dear to you. The
fact of losing brings with it a knowledge of what is much more
primitive, more emotional in nature. The new awareness says that
inherent in deciding to be involved, to care for someone, is the
understanding that you will have to give them up. And that losing
hurts. The life question then becomes, "Will I make myself vulnerable
again to this kind of pain?" A successfully resolved bereavement
affirms relationship and involvement in life despite the inherent
threat. It is better to love and care than to be emotionally insulated.
This is a miraculous decision when the bereaved emerges from the
pain of having lost prepared to reinvest in another relationship.

Further, there are no stages, formulas, or set patterns
which characterize the grief experience either for the person who
faces a terminal illness or for the survivor who has lost a loved one.
Elisabeth Kübler-Ross revolutionized our understanding of death and
dying with her delineation of stages she had observed in terminal

12. Reports of the President's Commission for the Study of Ethical Problems in
Medicine and Biomedical and Behavioral Research. U.S. Government Printing
Office, Washington, D.C.

patients.[13] Helping professionals became aware of denial, anger, bargaining, depression, and acceptance in grief work. Her work was a welcome change from traditional means of dealing with dying patients, which seldom went beyond notions of denial. However, her stages of death and dying, which she intended to be descriptive of common patterns, have now come to be prescriptive. Patients, pastors, and families often expect the individual to experience these stages in proper order with the proper time frame.

The work of Kübler-Ross is helpful. It is simply important not to take this as the only way to view the grief process of both patient and surviving family. A patient suffering from a terminal illness may experience many behaviors and feelings which are generally useful for helpers to understand. These feelings include shock, fear, numbness, guilt, anger, depression, lethargy, sadness, self-indulgence, and a host of others. They are normal, though not comfortable feelings. Nor is it unusual for seriously ill patients to consider suicide. While a few may actually attempt or complete a suicide, most contemplate it as a mechanism for staying in touch with a personal measure of control. In effect, "I can end this pain if I so choose. I am not helpless!" It can be therapeutic to affirm the patient's decision-making alternatives, including suicide. Once having acknowledged suicidal thoughts, the patient is usually able to move beyond that notion and into more positive coping devices. Acknowledging suicidal ideas, in and of itself, does not give permission for the patient to take his or her life. Behaviors usually range between the polarities of accepting or denying the realities of illness. This, too, is normal and the pastor should be prepared for wide variations in the patients' or families' focus on reality. Denial is destructive only when it threatens harm to relationships or necessary decision-making.

It was mentioned earlier that the resolution of bereavement usually requires several years, sometimes longer. The working through process is not in any sense mathematical. That is, a survivor does not steadily "feel better" in a measurable way. In recent years, Kübler-Ross' stages of death and dying have been applied to grief work as well. The same strengths and limitations which were mentioned in using these criteria with the dying patient may also apply to the grief work of the surviving family. While it is true that denial, bargaining, *etc.* may be part of the grief process, there is a danger that these may be taken as prescriptions for getting over the

---

13. E. Kübler-Ross, *On Death and Dying*, New York: Macmillan Publishing Co., Inc., 1969.

pain of death. There is an alternative image once shared with me by another pastor that many people who have suffered loss find extremely helpful. Consider the grief process to be like climbing a long winding staircase. You can move farther and farther from the source of that pain, but at any moment you can lean over the bannister and look back down to the source of that pain with a clarity that can throw off your balance all over again.

The image of the winding staircase is a good reminder that we never truly get over our deep losses. We may travel certain distances from them and they may fade as a prominent force in our lives, but they remain. This kind of understanding may be useful in working with people who have suffered significant loss.

Just because tears don't come as frequently is not an indicator that the pain has subsided. In fact, it may actually feel worse as time goes on. This can be very confusing and can make the grief-stricken person wonder if he or she is going "crazy." A usual approach to problem solving is to outline the concern, identify several solutions, and try one until it feels better. Grief is not so logical. Eventually it does get better, but for a while even feeling better can present problems. More clearly, a primitive notion can exist which says, "How can I allow myself to feel happy again when this person who was so special to me is dead?" The guilt is not real, but the person needs permission to enjoy life again. These are subtleties which caregivers must come to understand.

Finally, the training of the minister, as well as lay ministers within the church, must be on-going, especially as listening skills apply to persons experiencing life-threatening illness. Finding someone who hears with understanding and acceptance during crisis events is like discovering a treasure. It can feel more precious than gold. Particularly is this true when the listener does not respond with advice, cliches, or false assurance. In due time faith categories must be related to the life events which are being experienced. Using all these perspectives which are suggested as general guides, including the integration of faith categories, how does the pastor intervene in a sensitive way to the patient/family who will face dying because of serious illness or injury?

First, in the minister's orientation, it is helpful to know how the presence of a life-threatening event developed. An unexpected heart attack, or automobile accident, with the patient comatose and not expected to recover, presents a unique set of concerns as compared to the diagnosis of illness which will, in four or five years, cause the patient's death. There is no anticipatory grieving possible, no time to prepare by making amends or putting things in order in the relationship. Survivors are unusually vulnerable, both to psychological trauma and a sense of mortality. Feelings of guilt and anger as normal responses to loss are often intensified, perhaps to a level where they threaten to block the grief work, resulting in a pathological inability to reinvest emotionally in life.

Often, the trauma patient who will die from injuries sustained in an accident will be hospitalized in an intensive care unit. This may be a surgical, medical, coronary, or burn I.C.U. Visiting times will be limited to brief periods during the day. Between opportunities to visit, family members usually wait in an area of the hospital designated as an I.C.U. waiting area. It is an intensely anxious time since all the patients in these units are critically ill. All the family members present are tense and frequently on edge. Although I.C.U. patients are alert at times, they are often confused and/or comatose. Sometimes the confusion is caused by a combination of medications and what is called "I.C.U. psychosis," brought on by overstimulation of the senses.

Regardless, even if the patient is comatose, you can encourage family members to speak to the patient and share special feelings. It is entirely possible that at some level the patient is able to hear and understand what is being said. This can provide family members an opportunity to share some of the feelings and concerns which are otherwise so unfinished. During a visit which includes the pastor, prayer can become more meaningful when you consider that the patient's hearing allows participation.

In the case of a life-threatening diagnosis, the task of the patient and family is to struggle with shock and the needs to deny a harsh reality while at the same time making realistic decisions regarding treatment alternatives and life plan considerations. Frequently, this time is like having a thoroughgoing identity crisis. Questions such as "What am I worth?" "Who am I?" "How do I relate to my family?" are mentally and emotionally pondered if not spoken. There will be some well-intentioned, but misguided persons who will advise as to what ought to be done, provide newspaper clippings of "cures" discovered and being offered in faraway places, and who will falsely assure that "If you place your trust in God, everything will be O.K." Into this explosion of feelings and upset the pastor can, by presence and careful listening, begin to assist both patient and family to focus on the challenges which they face.

There are many religious issues to be encountered during the crisis of serious illness. All the thinking regarding the nature of humankind, God, and Creation which took place in cloistered halls of theological education take on the living, breathing intensity of clinging to a sense of meaning and purpose. My experience in hospitals suggests this kind of very fundamental struggle with faith.

One need of the patient/family is to retain a sense of God's presence with them. What the notion of "presence" means is hard to understand. Perhaps the antithesis of "abandonment" is a better feeling to initiate some appreciation for what "presence" might be like. At work among the emotional orientation of many Protestants is a primitive notion that during harsh, painful times, God is separated from you. It isn't an adult, rational response, but a very childlike notion that "if God really cared, then this wouldn't be happening."

That irrational feeling should not be confused with the very real notion that "this is not the way I wanted life to be." Such a response makes sense to all of us. As Allport[14] so wisely suggested, we must strive to update our faith so that it is in dialogue with reality, no matter how harsh. He spoke of maintaining firsthand fittings of faith. Isaiah 40:21-31 speaks so keenly to the nature of God during times of upset. It's wonderful to "soar with the eagles." But much of life is routine and utterly familiar so that the challenge is to "run and not grow weary." Unfortunately there are also times when life is so harsh, so painful, that getting to the next hour and not fainting is a monumental accomplishment. The assurance is that God will be in our midst during each of these times. No one of these situations is more authentic a way to experience life than is another, although we all prefer to "soar" whenever possible. God does not intervene to change "fainting" times to "soaring" times. Ultimately death comes as the master healer, to bring an end to suffering and a peace that could no longer be attained in life. I have noticed that "presence" is facilitated more easily for sacramental groups where rituals symbolically provide communion with God. Those ministers who rely on spoken words might be more attentive to the value of rituals.

Another frequent faith issue is that of the nature of Man and Creation. Perhaps Frankl[15] is as useful as anyone at this juncture. He recalls his deathcamp experiences and the horror of watching madness turned loose. In the midst of that trauma, however, he observed that some prisoners would survive while others, with similar circumstances, would die. The difference seemed to be that some clung to a meaning and hope in living. In the experience of serious illness, a crucial issue is living until you have to die. Few people die all at once. There comes a time when you can no longer jog, or walk, or get out of bed. But even those times can be extended. Another type of example is "when do you stop being a parent

---

14. G. Allport, *The Individual and His Religion*, New York: Macmillan Publishing Co., Inc., 1950.
15. V.E. Frankl, *Man's Search for Meaning*, New York: Pocket books, 1963.

because of serious illness?" You may not be able to play ball or do other active functions. But the will to meaning and purpose can keep you in touch with other ways of activating that role. This is a faith issue which every pastor should be prepared to share when the times are appropriate. Serious illness may not represent the way life ought to be. Despite it, however, man can continue to posit meaning and purpose, impacting positively upon creation.

Although coping styles vary immensely and every family system utilizes idiosyncratic rituals, there seem to be several behaviors which facilitate living with a serious illness. To be aware of these behaviors can provide a pastor with an assessment tool which further guides interventions. First, it is helpful if everyone, including patient and family, knows and understands the diagnosis, as well as prognostic information. "Everyone" includes children. It may be the case that a child's knowing and understanding may take a different shape than the adult or adolescent. The worst response, however, is to exclude them from significant involvement. Therefore, help the family get a clear statement of the nature of the illness from their physician.

Second it is important to have an open communication channel. Secrets between physician and patient, patient and family, or between family members require a misguided, wasteful use of energy. Inevitably, everyone learns what has been hidden, at which time resentment, anger, and fractured relationships result. Trust is built through learning that people can stand together, care for one another, and even grow in the face of adversity.

A third factor which facilitates adequate coping is that patient and family express appropriate affect. Simply stated, affect is to the emotions what speech is to thoughts. An example of inappropriate affect is when someone feels sad but looks happy, with smiles and greetings for everyone. Being able to share honestly what one feels, through tears as well as through laughter, is a strength that enhances a support system.

In addition to understanding diagnosis, open communication, and appropriate affect, the last criterion the pastor can utilize to evaluate adequate coping is contingency planning. Whichever member of the family becomes patient, that person usually is responsible for key roles in the everyday functioning of the family. To illustrate, perhaps Mom is the treasurer or Dad the social coordinator. As long as possible, it is important for the patient to retain key responsibilities. Planning is necessary, however, for the time when the patient can no longer fulfill those roles. Someone else must learn how to do those things. Other role shifts may be needed among family members, also. Simple though they may seem, these four characteristics represent a high level of functional intimacy. A pastor can carefully observe how a family relates to these coping skills and, where there are gaps, ministry might be focused in those directions. Remember, in most serious illnesses, there is time to grow and learn new, more adequate coping skills. No one ever learned how to communicate clearly overnight. But a serious illness might provide impetus to begin learning this skill.

Following the death of the patient, the pastor should make a point of calling on survivors approximately four to six weeks later. At this juncture, much of the business of settling the estate will be completed. Frequently, this is the time when the reality of the loss becomes most intense. Extended family have long since returned home from the funeral rituals, and the attention of the general community has turned to other things. Subtle pressures exist for the grief work to become more private and for the survivor to appear in public as if adjustment to loss has been accomplished. Such is not the case, however. It is the time when pastoral intervention is most needed. If the minister possesses the counseling skills, a once-per-week appointment with the family is appropriate. If not, then the pastor should become a bridge toward a referral source. Left alone, the family will become increasingly isolated in their bereavement.

Even if the minister refers to another helping professional, there are a number of thoughtful, sensitive opportunities for follow-up. Significant calendar dates are especially tender moments, particularly birthdays, wedding anniversaries, and the annual date of death. Seasons of the year bring their own emotions as well. The first several Thanksgivings, Christmases, and vacation periods present unique stress. These are family-oriented times which require reshaping once a significant other is no longer present. This may require several years before new and comfortable patterns emerge. The decision to attend church without the partner is also difficult. These occasions call for a special sensitivity.

For the children of a parent who dies, there may be particular difficulties with faith issues. The normal anger associated with loss may become focused on issues about God and Creation. For example, the notion that "God is love" may be disturbing as a child tries to solve the puzzle of a loving God, all powerful, who does not intervene to save a beloved parent even after much prayer. Adults struggle with this issue more than we are willing to acknowledge. Living with realities such as the world not being a fair place, or necessarily reflective of justice, poses serious theological questions. Be patient and loving with these children as their hurts will be with them for a lifetime. They will remember always your interventions. Better they hold to an image of your kindness and warm touch than that you attempted to persuade them with theological apologetics. In time they will be developmentally able to deal with life's subtleties and incongruities. One hopes that, at that time, they will have a pastor as sensitive as you who can harvest the good seeds you planted.

The experience of serious illness which shortens life presents a challenge to the skills of the pastor. It is a life experience which requires unique coping skills from both patient and family. And, it requires continuing adjustment for the survivors extending several years beyond the death of the loved one. Among the helping professionals, perhaps no person is in a better position to provide ongoing care than is the minister. The suggestions in this chapter can provide some useful guidelines.

Rituals of Faith and Particular Practices

It is not uncommon for the pastor to enact the rituals of faith during a visit to the hospital. Sometimes it will be known ahead of time that communion, for example, is desired by the patient. On other occasions, requests may occur during the visit. Some of these rituals may require either special facilities or permission for the patient to participate in them. Most are best celebrated with the assurance of privacy. Hospital staff will respect the wishes of the patient for these rituals, particularly if they have been informed about what is planned. On many occasions, they will see such an event as a special opportunity which staff can participate in as well.

As an example, imagine that a parishioner has contacted you regarding dedicating a new baby while mother and child are still in the hospital. The first thing to do is to meet with the parents, perhaps including the nursing supervisor on that unit. If the supervisor is not included, that person should be consulted before any plans are finalized. The staff on the patient's floor will almost always assist you in finding a time when there can be privacy, but some would probably be interested in attending the dedication if you and the patient are willing. This would apply to requests for special prayers, baptisms, and communion. The latter has the added dimension of checking to make sure the patient can ingest the elements.

Even when the patient's request involves extraordinary features, communication and planning with the hospital staff can make possible what is needed. For example, a patient recently requested to be baptized by immersion. The pastor involved worked closely with both the patient's physician and the nursing coordinator. It was decided that the patient could be transported to the Physical

Therapy area and a Hubbard tank was utilized to perform the baptism. This story circulated throughout the hospital for several days and staff, particularly, felt a unique sense of accomplishment that they had been involved in making it possible. The key was a sensitive pastor who asked for help in order to be able to assist a patient.

In a similar fashion, ministers representing faith groups who have practices which are not commonly known will generally experience the same kind of acceptance and cooperation if time is taken to communicate with staff what the patient requires in order to observe the practices of that faith. Deliverance counselors utilizing exorcism, persons speaking in tongues, the laying on of hands, anointing with oil, circumcision, and prayers for the dying can all find opportunity for expression if care is taken to inform and prepare. Again, this is the minister's or rabbi's responsibility. The hospital will usually have at least two specific concerns: first, there must be no harm, injury, or any detrimental effect upon the patient's treatment or recovery. This kind of concern grows out of those rare negative instances where, for example, a pastor insisted that a patient incapable of doing so get out of bed and on his knees in order to pray. Second, because hospitals cannot provide privacy like being in your own home, any procedure or event involving one patient can involve at least one other person, perhaps more. Respecting the privacy of all patients is important. Consequently, a ritual of faith involving speaking in tongues can be accomplished as far as the hospital is concerned, but only after the participating patient has been moved to a private space.

American blacks are often very expressive of grief following the death of a loved one. Anticipating this, the black pastor can communicate with hospital staff to help them understand the normalcy of this response. Compared to most persons staff is exposed to, the black response is unusual. Actually it is more healthy than the typical abbreviated or restrained response more commonly seen. Not necessarily being aware of this as a normal response, however, the staff might automatically prescribe a sedative or tranquilizer. If the pastor prepares staff, a more private space can be arranged where the feelings can be unobtrusively shared. The chanting of ritual prayers by a Hindu or Muslim priest presents a similar concern and probable solution.

With some exceptions, hospitals are cultural melting pots with a variety of belief systems and philosophic orientations represented among the patients. Examples of exceptions might be a Jewish hospital in a large metropolitan area or a Catholic hospital, where symbols of each faith group might be prominent. Even in these exceptions, however, hospitals respect the ecumenical nature of their patient population and do everything possible to facilitate the patient utilizing the resources of a particular faith system. The pastor, priest, or rabbi will almost always experience cooperation if he or she takes time to communicate, including demonstrating a respect for the limits of the patient-parishioner and the privacy of other non-parishioner-patients.

There are times when the practices of certain religious groups conflict with standard medical procedure. The media focus attention on the extreme cases, and such publicity often sets the stage for mutual distrust between hospitals and members of these religious groups. For the most part, however, conflict can be minimized when proper procedures are followed. The following guidelines use Jehovah's Witnesses, Christian Science, and Seventh Day Adventists as examples of the ways hospitals and these religious groups have developed arenas of mutual concern and understanding.

The law recognizes the right of a competent person of legal age to refuse certain medical treatment, even if that medical treatment would be life saving. This decision is not based on the right to refuse treatment, but on the right to privacy, which is an ethical/legal principle established in the Karen Quinlan case. For a Christian Scientist, this means that an adult with competency to decide may retain control of what medical procedures he or she would allow. In fact certain legal precedents indicate that medical treatment of a competent adult against his or her will may constitute assault.

Beyond legal restraints, physicians also realize that their treatment may be detrimental if it does not respect the spiritual as well as physical well-being of the patient. For example, Jehovah's Witnesses conscientiously oppose the use of blood transfusions. This includes the taking of a patient's blood prior to surgery and reserving it for use with that patient. A patient's blood is not to be separated from the circulatory system. Hospitals which recognize the legal restraints here but also seek ways to treat people with this conviction have developed equipment which can purify and replenish the blood supply for Jehovah's Witnesses without violating their religious belief.[16] Not only have many hospitals refined their techniques for such treatment, but they have also increased their studies of the risks of such procedures in comparison to control groups. Such studies have indicated that among Jehovah's Witnesses alternative treatments

---

16. Richard F. Kaplan et al., "Transfusions for Jehovah's Witnesses," *Anesthesiology Analogue*, 1983, 62:122–26.

for blood replenishment handled with due precaution result in minimal risk of morbidity and mortality when compared with control groups.[17]

Another level of concern is that of Seventh Day Adventists, who have dietary restrictions. Certain meats are considered unclean, and many Seventh Day Adventists are vegetarians. A patient with these dietary convictions may experience considerable anxiety entering a hospital if he or she is unsure of how these convictions will be respected. An important role for you as clergy is to help the patient understand that these beliefs will be honored, but the patient must deal with the appropriate hospital official. Help the patient consult with the dietician, not the orderly who delivers the food, and there should be no problem.

While the law recognizes the right of competent adults to refuse medical treatment, the situation changes somewhat in the case of children and emergencies where the patient is comatose, confused, or incapable of making an informed decision. In the case of children (minors) from either Christian Science or Jehovah's Witnesses where the health and well-being of a child is in danger, the hospital would seek temporary guardianship of the child in the courts. Most arguments by hospitals that a parental belief cannot be imposed upon a child when that belief would threaten the life of the child have been successful. In an emergency situation, when an adult is considered incompetent, standard medical treatment would be given.

Your role with patients from religious groups where certain medical practices are prohibited is to help the patient maintain clear communication with hospital administration on the treatment policy for the patient. Be familiar with current literature on the subject. Understand that most hospitals will cooperate with a patient's religious beliefs up to the point that these beliefs conflict with their own legal liability.

Psychiatric Hospitalization

Sooner or later, virtually every minister becomes involved in a situation where (s)he is called upon to assist in admitting someone to a psychiatric unit or to visit someone in such a unit. A member of your congregation living alone may be sinking into a suicidal depression, and you may be the only person able to get her to a hospital. You may be confronted with a transient who is clearly delusional, perhaps dangerous to you and others in the community, and the responsibility for seeking psychiatric care for this person may fall on you. A church member may suffer a paranoia that is rendering him incapable of functioning with his family or at his work, and both employer and

---

17. Mostaf I. Bonakdar et al., "Major Gynecologic and Obstetric Surgery in Jehovah's Witnesses," *Obstetrics and Gynecology*, 60(5), Nov. 1982, 587–590.

wife may ask you to convince him he needs hospital care. A young person, a long way from home, may find the pressure too much to bear. Suddenly his contact with reality breaks. He believes there are dangerous forces pursuing him. You are the person whose house he appears at in the middle of the night, and you must act.

To call these situations difficult is an understatement. Hospitalizing someone is almost always a negative experience. The individual may resist. Hospital admitting staff may well see the situation differently than you. One pastoral counselor said that these are the times that make you question the decision to enter the ministry.

This section will provide a framework for understanding the process of hospitalizing an individual for psychiatric reasons. It will also offer guidelines for visiting a person who is a patient in a psychiatric hospital.

There are two factors which are important to all aspects of psychiatric hospitalization. The first is to be in contact with other mental health professionals. It is critical that you develop a support system of other counselors before you face the crisis of hospitalizing someone. A social worker, accredited pastoral counselor, psychologist, or psychiatrist are all excellent resources for referral and support in this decision. It is important to have some connection with a psychiatrist, or psychologist for it is generally their evaluation which will finally determine if an individual will be committed to a psychiatric unit or hospital.

The second factor is to be familiar with legal statutes and hospital criteria for psychiatric hospitalization. State laws for involuntary hospitalization usually require that an individual be dangerous to himself or others. This means a person must be suicidal, physically destructive, or potentially violent. The violence toward others, however, must stem from a psychotic or delusional condition. Admitting psychiatrists are not willing to use psychiatric units as substitutes for jails.

Once you are familiar with the law and have made contact with a psychiatrist and other counselors who can assist you in future emergencies, be aware of your instincts in this arena. Some ministers have a tendency to think they can handle all crises themselves. One clinical psychologist in a rural mental health clinic said that ministers in her area tend to wait too long before referring a person for hospitalization. They refuse to recognize that a person is in deeper trouble than they can handle. Families and churches too often try to absorb bizarre behavior. This psychologist maintains that quicker intervention would make the treatment easier on the patient. Each of us has a certain blind side, a tendency toward excess. If yours is to wait too long before you consider hospitalization, then enlist another minister or trusted counselor to consult with when you confront a difficult situation. Ask this professional if it is time to consider hospitalization and listen to the feedback.

Of course many ministers have the opposite tendency, which is to refer a person for hospitalization too soon. Another psychologist, this time a director of a university counselling center, said that he often sees helping professionals, including ministers, turning to hospitalization too soon. He asks that community counselors and ministers make more use of families and other support systems, realizing that hospitalization should only be considered as a last resort. Therefore, beware of this tendency as well. Use the same system of consulting with other professionals before you begin the hospitalization process.

What criteria should you use to determine if hospitalization is necessary? The clearest signal is if a person is speaking of suicide. This should always be taken seriously, but such talk does not always suggest the need for hospitalization. It should be considered dangerous if the individual indicates having the means to carry out the suicide threat. Listen for specifics. How dangerous are the methods for suicide the person suggests or describes? How available are these means? Take all threats seriously and consult with other professionals, sharing the lethality and accessibility of the means described. A local suicide and crisis center is an excellent resource in times when you need help in making a judgment such as whether to hospitalize someone talking of suicide.

The other extreme behavior warranting hospitalization is behavior which is violent toward others. Violent, uncontrollable behavior in unexplainable and irrational cycles should not be handled alone. Seek assistance from other professionals in admitting violent individuals for psychiatric hospitalization.

Once you have decided to admit someone for psychiatric care, it is often best to contact the admitting psychiatrist or psychologist ahead of time and share your perspectives. Have a concrete list of bizarre behaviors or thought patterns. The individual you bring to the hospital may suddenly become calm and orderly in front of the admitting doctor. This person in charge of admission does not have easy access to important data, so you must be prepared to offer examples of the behavior in question.

While it is true that ministers sometimes wait too long to obtain psychiatric help for individuals in need, it must be remembered that hospitalization is viewed as the last resort by all professionals. Hospital personnel often do not see or hear the individual's symptoms in the same way you have. After all the trauma of convincing a person to go to the hospital, you may be turned away. Be prepared for this possibility. Have other options to turn to if admission is denied. These options may be family, half-way houses, even daily outpatient therapy.

Psychiatric hospitalization is generally carried out through the hospital emergency room, an outpatient clinic, or a community mental health center. If the hospital has a psychiatric unit, a psychiatric professional will generally be on call. If the hospital rejects the person, then go back to the admissions person or the mental health center and develop a mutually acceptable program of therapy.

If the person is admitted to the hospital, the next step is determining your role as a visitor on the psychiatric unit. Even if you brought the patient for admission, you may find yourself cut off from further contact with this individual. This may be frightening and frustrating, for you may now worry about the condition of someone you entrusted to the hospital.

At this point, it is important to understand that the first task of the psychiatric staff is to stabilize the individual who is now their patient. Often this means reducing outside stimuli. Often even immediate family are kept away or extremely limited in visits. If you cannot see the patient immediately, talk to the psychiatrist in charge of the case and see what you can do. I know of one minister who was told to bake cookies for a patient he could not yet visit. This was not a superficial dismissal. It was a concrete way the minister could send a symbol of continued care and concern. This may be the most positive ministry one can have when a person is first admitted for psychiatric hospitalization.

When you are allowed to visit, again find out what kind of communication is appropriate. Reassure the hospital staff that you can be part of an extended support system.

Begin with short visits. Accept that you are not to be a therapist. Be prepared for confusing and contradictory responses from the patient. The patient may be hostile or sullen. But it is important for the patient to know that there is someone who cares and even accepts this unorthodox behavior. This is the time for you to have the courage to be there, without trying to provide a solution for the patient's problems. Reassure the patient of your continued support and offer hope. Accept the confusion of the moment. Keep in touch with the staff. While you should accept the restrictions the hospital staff may place on early visits, it is also important to remain assertive in obtaining the information you need to maintain your role as pastor.

What about the role of the church at large? This is a difficult dilemma, for there are the competing concerns of confidentiality and support. Generally, confidentiality is the number one priority. Unless a patient or family releases you to contact other members of the church for support, the privacy of the patient should be respected. Sometimes a few close friends will be aware of what is happening and may consult with you for ways to be helpful. Other times the psychiatric hospitalization will be something a number of people become aware of. In both cases, it is often best to offer gentle and respectful support for an individual who is in a psychiatric unit. Again, the symbol of baking cookies is good. Gestures of care and concern which are simple and non-intrusive are often the best.

I want to offer one footnote on dealing with psychosis. It has been said that neurotics build castles in the sky, and psychotics live in them. A neurotic person has difficulties at times distinguishing between fantasy and reality, but a psychotic is living in an altered state. Psychotic people live in a different reality. Listen to psychotics according to all the best rules of counselling. Talk to them about their delusions and how they see what they see. At some point, gently begin talking to them about resources that are available to help them through their pain, resources such as a psychiatric hospital. Reassure them that such places will not harm them.

Making this transition from listening to referral will not be easy, and it will be important for you to maintain your sense of confidence. Psychotic people have an uncanny ability to sense your vulnerability and manipulate you from that place. If they perceive that your age, sex, or race causes you any insecurity, they may exploit this as a sign of lack of authority. They may play on your religious convictions to avoid dealing with therapeutic issues. If you harbor a guilt about hospitalizing people, they may spot this and capitalize on it.

Realize what is happening. Stay firm. Call in other clergy, counselors, the mental health center, or the hospital emergency room whenever you need assistance. Everyone is vulnerable somewhere, and this arena of ministry brings hidden vulnerabilities right to the surface.

In summary, there are three basic guidelines to follow in dealing with psychiatric hospitalization. First, be familiar with the criteria and procedures for hospitalization. Second, develop good contacts with psychiatrists, psychologists, and other mental health professionals. Do not try to handle these situations alone. Develop your structure of support before you need it so it will be available when you need it. Third, follow good professional standards of listening, limiting what you try to do, and accepting the patient just as you would in any other hospital situation.

Hospitalization and the Adolescent — A Systems Approach   Adolescence is a particularly dangerous time in the human life cycle. Adolescent boys are often categorized as an "at risk" population, having twice the death rate of adolescent girls. In fact, until very recently, teenagers were the only age group in America for whom death rates were increasing. (David Hamburg, "Preparing for Life: the Critical Transition of Adolescence," reprinted from the 1986 Annual Report of the Carnegie Corporation of New York, 437 Madison Ave., New York, N.Y.) When we see adolescents in the hospital it is likely to be as the result of an injury due to an accident, a suicide attempt, drug or substance abuse, anti-social behavior, or even as the result of sexual or physical assault or abuse. Often this will involve psychiatric hospitalization.

Hospitals, like society, are confused about where to place adolescents. Teenagers may wind up surrounded by clown wallpaper and crying children in a pediatric unit. They may be equally uncomfortable sharing the room with an elderly gall bladder patient. Psychiatric hospitals are of varying quality, and suddenly there is a new wave of private psychiatric facilities designed just for adolescents for which common standards of evaluation are still not set.

As a result of all these factors, visiting the adolescent patient is different from visiting either an adult or a child. Understanding the nature of the condition requiring hospitalization, the unique needs of the hospitalized individual, and the family situation of the patient, is always important in hospital visitation. But these factors are especially crucial in a hospital ministry to adolescents. Therefore, we approach this visitation of the adolescent as part of a family/church system.

One way to understand the situation in which the adolescent finds him or herself is by seeing the entire system of the adolescent, the family, and the church as a developmental irony. Teenagers themselves find their situation ironic in that every part of their life seems to be in a double bind. Their senses are perhaps more alert than any other time in life, but their lack of judgment makes driving an automobile a risky business according to insurance statistics. Adolescents feel the strong desire for independence, yet they do not have the means of financial support necessary to live alone. As one comedian put it, all their hormones are saying "Yes! Yes! Yes!" while every system around them — parent, school, and church — is saying, "No! No! No!". And for good reason.

Parents are part of this developmental irony. Parents who assume they have learned some skills in parenting often report being transported to the same confusing time as parenting a two year old. The flowering of youth occurs in the confusion of mid-life for parents. These stages are volatile for both parent and child. Ellen Galinksy in her book *Between Generations: The Six Stages of Parenthood* says "The teenager is a constant reminder that the parent is working at something (staying young) that the teenager has easily in her grasp."

Middle age parents are caught in three generational cycles, between the needs of teenage children which are not only more complex than they used to be but which cost a lot more too, the increasing problems and needs of their own parents in the grandparent generation, and their own middle age.

Finally the parent has the task of allowing a child to separate while at the same time creating new ties which will last through the coming generation of adulthood. The child's need to separate from the parent stirs up feelings of envy, fear, hostility, and nostalgia. At the same the separate achievements of the child create pride, a real glow of parenting and the sense of new freedom of life that lies ahead for both parent and child.

I have spoken of the developmental ironies of the teenage years in parent/child terms because they are the clearest and most personal ways to see and understand them. These ironies are mirrored in the church or religious community. Just when the young person may truly need a place or institution that is his or her own, the church is identified as belonging to the parents. While the church may turn out to be one institution that can reach out with genuine care, adolescent individuation may cause the young person to turn his back on that care.

Edwin Friedman, a rabbi and psychiatrist from Washington, D.C. says that we carry our patterns of behavior from our family of origin, to our nuclear family, to the family that is our church. (*Generation to Generation*, Guilford Press, N.Y. 1985)

It is important for us as clergy and helpers to realize the degree to which we carry our own experiences as teenagers into our parenting of our own teenagers and our dealing with teenagers in the church. Those of us who found adolescence a painful time which we would rather forget than relive probably do not invest ourselves heavily with the youth of our church. Those of us who found youth group the best years of our lives probably have a difficult time ever getting beyond being youth ministers. Those of us who first discerned our sense of ministry as a vocation when we were teenagers have deep emotional investments in this age of life. And if we have teenagers at home, our ups and downs with them may well bleed into the ways we deal with not only the young people but the whole congregation.

The same is true of our congregation. The difficulties of dealing with teenagers in the church are often just the clearest symptoms of difficulties in the whole system of a family with teenagers.

Consider the stakes. Many people join the church so their children will grow up in a positive environment. They invest quite a lot in providing a faith community for teenagers to find their own faith in particular. But see the contradiction right there? The healthiest faith has to be owned by the individual, yet the parent and the church all want it to grow in their community.

Here we begin to see some of the issues in dealing with the troubled teenager. The pendulum of emotions will swing steadily between freedom and dependence on everyone's part. A young person angry at his or her parents may act this out by rebelling against the church. Parents upset with their children may sabotage their participation in church youth programs.

The cycle is endless. The point here is that when problems arise in dealing with teenagers in the religious community, it is seldom a problem of the teenagers alone. Families easily make teenagers the "identified patient", the scapegoat for family dysfunction. When you are called in to help sort out the inevitable problems of the teenage years, remember that this is a systemic, not an individual issue.

Ministry to the adolescent, just like adolescent life itself, walks a tightrope of separation and connection, challenge and acceptance, old wisdom and new discovery. It is the loss of balance on this tightrope that often puts the adolescent in the hospital. It is therefore crucial that caregivers understand how to rebalance this young person in order that he or she may continue this precarious journal to a new platform of safety.

What then is your role in dealing with a hospitalized teenager and the church? This is a difficult issue to understand. David Viscott in his book *The Making of a Psychiatrist* says that much "normal" teenage behavior would be grounds for hospitalization in an adult. Just stop and watch a group of high school kids messing around before or after a church group meeting. The same behavior in adults would be downright bizarre. Therefore while even healthy teenage behavior may appear problematic to the adult eye, it is important to distinguish specific behaviors and situations which are likely to result in hospitalization for teenagers. Six signs and symptoms of troubled teenagers are listed below. Each holds opportunities for intervention, but any may well lead to hospitalization.

After listing these six signs and symptoms we will discuss the specifics of hospital visitation in these circumstances.

1. *Anti-social acting out.* This is a common description of the behavior of a troubled young person. Every youth group has a clown. The clown aspect is also easily reinforced by the group itself. While it is a funny role, it is also lonely. You as a leader may want to intervene with the youth leadership and even key members of the church to deliberately reinforce a moderation in behavior which does not destroy the individuality of the clown.

If the clown behavior is more than just cutting up, but evolves into minor vandalism, joy-riding in the car without permission from time to time, and occasional school truancy, this is the sign to contact a good family counselor and help the young person work through a process of redirecting positive energy. When the behavior becomes potentially or actually destructive to the teenager or others, some kind of residential treatment may be required.

The anti-social, or what used to be called the "delinquent" adolescent is clearly an individual in need. However, the opposite counterpoint, the "perfect" young person may also be at risk. Unfortunately churches tend to reinforce young people who act like little preachers. The young person who is "too good to be true", memorizing bible verses, never joining in the horseplay of his or her peers, may be just as much of a candidate for somatic symptoms, allergies, anorexia, as the anti-social young person is a candidate for danger with the law.

2. *The abused young person.* This is very tricky in the church. While child abuse is something we typically believe to occur in other families, certainly those outside our congregations, the statistics suggest that it is occurring in virtually every community including churches. Stay alert to physical symptoms, but more important, be aware of the emotional signs of abuse.

Unfortunately, sexual abuse is present in families and organizations of every racial, economic, and religious category. Girls and boys are abused by family members, as well as adults who have gained their trust as scout leaders, youth group directors, and coaches. When a young person in your group undergoes a sudden behavioral change, expressing anger, withdrawal, sullenness, aggressiveness, be sensitive to these as signs of an abusive situation.

As pastor to the family, your responsibilities are complicated. Many states have laws requiring that clergy report any abuse to the appropriate agency. Regardless of the legal requirements, it is important that we stay with the family to make sure they get supportive counselling. Above all we must protect the young person.

A young person who has been severely abused may be removed from that family while the dispute over the abuse and a treatment plan for family members is being developed. If the physical abuse has been severe, a young person may be admitted to a general hospital. If the wounds are emotional and psychological, the young person may be referred to a state social services network.

3. *Drugs and substance abuse.* Drugs are everywhere for young people. So is anti-drug hysteria. Good drug education is a must. But not all drug treatment and education programs are equal. It is very important for any pastor dealing with drug and substance abuse treatment teams to be informed.

This arena is one of the most common paths to hospitalization for teenagers today. Many private, for profit hospitals run expensive drug treatment centers for adolescents. It is important to visit any facilities which might be used by your church members. Get opinions from the wider counselling community about their treatment programs.

Since private insurance carriers will pay in the tens of thousands of dollars a month for treatment in these centers, it is now unfortunately the case that young people with drug or emotional problems represent potential income for these facilities. Most of these hospitals are excellent and well-staffed. Yet there are some programs and hospital facilities which will exploit young people in trouble. As a pastor, you can help family members discern the difference between good and bad.

Here are some specific questions you and a family may ask of any psychiatric treatment facility:

a. What kind of treatment program is offered? Ask for a treatment plan with concrete goals and objectives which are readily understandable. Find out how you will know when an objective is met. Ask the staff to outline a typical week in significant detail.

Is the staff trained in family therapy? This is an important element in modern treatment of teenagers. Find out if family participation is required. It should be. How is reentry into the family facilitated? Are there family weekends and times when the family is educated about follow-up?

b. Is a combination of individual and group therapy part of the treatment plan? Both are important.

c. Are quality activity therapies offered? Activities should be more than "basket making" busy work. A good activity program will have a certified occupational therapist in charge of a program with stated treatment objectives.

Is aerobic physical exercise included in the activities? Teenagers need good physical exercise.

d.   Is the facility accredited? The standard accreditation body is the JCAH (Joint Committee on the Accreditation of Hospitals). Membership in the National Association of Private Psychiatric Hospitals also indicates a quality program.

e.   What arrangements are made for schooling? Many facilities depend on teachers in a homebound program from the local school system. This is sufficient only if the hospitalization is short term, for one to two hours a day is not adequate schooling. If short-term schooling is all that is possible, contact the local school system's pupil personnel services and ask how well the institution cooperates in this program.

If hospitalization is long term, there should be an organized school program. If such a program exists, what affiliation does it have with regional or national organizations?

f.   What is the staff - patient ratio? Realize that 2 to 2 ½ employees to a patient is an industry standard. But this means every employee, including janitors and food service. A better question is therapist to patient ratio. General industry standards recommend a ratio of one therapist to eight to ten patients, although this may fluctuate somewhat with the patient census.

g.   What is the statement of patient rights? You should see a statement of patient rights and responsibilities. Substance abuse programs in particular may specifically limit patient rights and community contact in the beginning of a program. Parents may not be allowed to see their child, but even so there should be a clear statement of parental access to staff.

h.   Ask for a statement on their philosophy and policy of medication and review this with a counselling professional outside the institution.

This is the time and place to assist the family in determining privileges of phone calls and visitation. If the family does not designate clergy as having phone or visiting privileges, you may not be allowed access to the patient.

4.   *The divorce of a parent.* Only the death of a parent is more traumatic than divorce. Sometimes divorce can be even more difficult for a young person to deal with than death because its effects just refuse to go away. Clergy spend a lot of time with divorcing couples. Similar attention should be given to children, especially teenagers.

Many adolescents respond to the pain of divorce by holding back their feelings. This makes traditional individual counselling frustrating. It is very tempting to leave the adolescents to their moods and deal with family members who appear much more open to support. It is often true that you can only work with those people who want to work through their issue. If the adolescent does not want to deal with the issue of divorced parents, you cannot force her into counselling. However, there are many alternative ways of staying connected with the adolescent during this troubled time. Activities as specific as a children of divorce group can be organized in a church. Or your role may be as general as taking the young person out for ice cream just to touch base. The point is not to forget the pain of the adolescent in this difficult time.

Adolescents may withdraw from the family and invest heavily in other activities. This investment may be the church, or the church may be identified with the family and the young person will invest in another organization. The church has to be sensitive here, neither to exploit the young person or abandon him or her.

Also realize again that divorce can be the occasion for depression, anti-social behavior, even attempted suicide. Hospitalization again is a possibility for a young person going through this turmoil. Here the family system must be addressed, and clergy may be the only people in a position to do this. Feuding divorced parents may have to be confronted with the need to deal with their differences through a mature mediating process for the sake of enabling their child to become functional again.

5. *Suicidal behavior.* Suicide is still one of the primary causes of death among young people and is typically a prevalent reason for psychiatric hospitalization. Any young person who expresses suicidal behavior needs to be taken seriously. Just as we mentioned in the earlier part of this chapter on psychiatric hospitalization, the guidelines for referral usually mirror the lethality of the threat. Pay attention to the different needs expressed by someone who says "I think I'll kill myself" because he doesn't have a date and someone who makes specific descriptions of how he would in fact end his life.

It is extremely important to get help for yourself as soon as you feel any concern over a young person's suicidal behavior. You can use professional therapists at three levels. First, they can consult with you in your primary handling of the person. Second, you can make a referral to that professional. Third, the professional can help you in hospitalizing the young person if this is necessary and make sure they receive appropriate treatment.

Keep in mind that when a suicide, a suicide attempt, or any tragic event occurs in or close to a young person's peer group, it is important to take time to follow up on its impact with these young people in the peer group. Such events are often catching. When the unthinkable happens, it suddenly becomes thinkable. It is therefore very important to work through the meaning of tragedy for the peer group.

All of the above situations can result in hospitalization. But all adolescent hospitalization is not necessarily psychiatric hospitalization. Visiting an adolescent in a general hospital begins just like any other visit. Routine illnesses and procedures may be treated much the same way they would be treated in any patient. Since adolescents hover between childhood and adulthood, you need to be ready to turn your visit in either direction. On one day the adolescent patient might enjoy playing a game or watching a TV show with you. On another day that same adolescent might want to engage in a serious talk. There is no predicting either path. Be ready for both.

We have emphasized the important of data gathering for every kind of hospital visit. With the adolescent, include a systems approach in the data gathering. How does this particular hospitalization fit into the entire life situation? Does an injury or illness reflect any of the warning signs of the troubled adolescent described above? Does this hospitalization seem to be the result of anti-social acting out, pressure to conform, physical or sexual abuse, substance abuse, family trauma such as divorce, covert suicidal behavior, or a reaction to a tragedy in the peer group? If so, follow up counselling and referral is in order.

Be careful and sensitive here. The sudden awareness of the prevalence of physical abuse, drug abuse, and the threat of suicide has meant that young people are constantly questioned about their involvement in these arenas. You do not want to miss important cues. Yet you do not want to suggest that these problems exist where there are none.

Take your cues from the patient. Resist the temptation to preach, which is easy to get into with young people. Offer the spiritual support appropriate to the situation. Gentle prayers and hopeful visions are good ways to enable the young person to see his future as one of health and healing.

When a teenager has been injured, or hurt herself, other adolescents are often the best support system. Here the clergy can train other teenagers to be peer counselors in helping friends recover from trauma. Peer counselling has been identified by David Hamburg in the 1986 Carnegie Report as the single most effective intervention for adolescents. High school and mental health counselors in most communities have training in developing peer counselling programs. Simple training in active listening and non-judgmental support can give teenagers the tools they need to be a healing presence. It is important to stay very closely involved with young people who act as a support system for their injured friends. Be a supervisor to them as they support others.

A teenager may also be committed to some form of psychiatric hospitalization. The first thing to do here is find out from the facility what arrangements exist for the visit of a pastor. As we mentioned earlier, almost all psychiatric facilities begin their treatment by limiting outside stimuli for their patients. The first reaction a pastor may receive from staff might be very negative. It is important, therefore, that you meet with the supervisor of your parishioner and find out exactly how you will be able to participate in the healing process.

The patient and family may be embarrassed by the situation which has caused the young person to be hospitalized. You will need to reassure everyone of your respect for their privacy and your continuing support.

As you are admitted into the facility and able to visit the young person, find out what kind of behavior is considered appropriate for the teenager. Given your limits, ask the young person what kinds of magazines, foods, books, or video games he might like.

Since you will be one of the first persons other than family from the outside, your treatment will be very important. Natural, matter of fact, easy going behavior is the most therapeutic. This patient has the necessary psychiatric team for in depth counselling. You do not need to do this.

It is important to stay in close touch with the people at the institution who are the decision makers. I had a situation where I had cleared all the channels to visit a young person at a private psychiatric facility. The people at the hospital knew me. I had spoken to his caseworker, and the appointment was set. When I arrived the caseworker told me the young person had tried to run away the night before and would not be allowed to see me. Different reasons were given to me for not allowing the visit. But none were absolutely clear. I also was unable to find anyone in authority to talk to.

I called the administrator the next day, upset for a number of reasons. First, I was worried about the patient himself and the mixed messages I was receiving about him and why I could not see him. Secondly, I had driven quite a distance. Since I had an appointment, I felt someone could have notified me not to come.

The administrator was helpful and understanding. I called before leaving my office for the next visit. When I arrived the young person was already waiting for me in a visiting room. We had a good visit. Everyone was most cooperative.

It is also important to stay in touch with family members. Privacy is a difficult issue. A family who tells no one that a child is in a psychiatric facility will feel very much alone. Helping that family confide in trusted friends at the right time can open the doors to care and support.

It is also true that members of the young person's peer group can again be the most helpful parties in recovery. When family and professionals agree that it is time for contact with other young people, appropriate friends can be brought into the picture. At first this might be through a card signed by youth group members. Then specific letters can be sent or a phone call made. When the patient has earned visiting privileges, young people can go see her. Finally, most residential treatment programs begin release with temporary passes or furloughs. Here contact with healthy friends can be the most important step back into the outside world.

The complexity of dealing with the hospitalized teenager may seem overwhelming. We may quickly feel we just do not have the expertise to help a sexually abused teenager, or the victim of a drug overdose.

Here is where I suggest that being a general practitioner is a gift. Realize we do the greatest harm when we think we are experts. We also suffer from messianic delusions, thinking that God has no other hands and feet than ours. That of course is patently ridiculous.

In one of my days of mid-life melancholy, I realized that I was really an expert at nothing in my church. In my church there are people who are better teachers than I, better administrators, better speakers, better theologians, better business-people, and better counselors. Every time I go to a continuing education seminar on something like family therapy, I think, "I should get really good at this." Then I go to a church administration seminar, and I think, "I should get really good at this." Then I go to bible study training, and the same thing happens.

I finally accepted that I am going to be general practitioner of ministry at all these things. But by being a general practitioner rather than a specialist, I am also able to put all these skills together in a church very well. In fact nobody in my church quite puts them together as I do. I can feel good about that.

When a special problem leading to the psychiatric hospitalization of a teenager comes along, we need to look to our gifts as general practitioners. What do general practitioners do? First we do our homework, calling specialists, reading a few articles so we know what we are facing. Then we move in to keep an eye on the whole picture. While one person may be treating the patient for a physical wound, another considering emotional trauma, and another balancing legal and financial questions, we are in a situation to address all of these issues. Finally, we are a link from patient, to family, to church, to community.

To see the whole picture and treat the whole person in a way which nobody else does is the gift of the general practitioner of ministry. Being a general practitioner is not an excuse to be sloppy in our diagnosis or careless in our work. Rather it is a challenge to do what we do best, keeping the whole person, body and spirit, living as an individual in a community, in mind. Ministering to the hospitalized adolescent is just one of the many arenas in which we exercise this ministry.

Bibliography

Caine, L. *Widow*. New York: Bantam Books, 1975.
The author shares her personal experience of adjusting to the death of her husband. The book is excellent in terms of providing a real life experience for the reader. Ministers in general are not presented in a positive light. If this dimension can be overlooked, it is a useful book.

Charry, Dana. *Mental Health Skills for Clergy*. Valley Forge, Pa.: Judson Press, 1982.
Helpful in determining suicidal threats, signs of depression, how to handle referrals.

Claypool, J.R. *Tracks of a Fellow Struggle: How to Handle Grief*. Waco, Texas: Word Press, 1974.
A very sensitive and profound sharing by an articulate pastor who allows the reader to re-trace the agony of his daughter's serious illness and death from leukemia. This book can be useful to both ministers and lay persons; for churches developing lay-helper programs, the issues discussed in this book would provide for many hours of productive discussion.

Clements, W.M. "Reminiscence as the Cure of Souls in Early Old Age." *Journal of Religion and Health* Vol. 20(1), Spring 1981, pp. 41–47.
A very helpful article for ministers and lay persons who have an interest in the elderly. The article focuses on the subject of 'storytelling' and its curative value to persons whose range of acquaintances is growing ever narrower.

Dobihal, E.F. and Stewart, C.W. *When a Friend is Dying*. Nashville: Abingdon Press, 1984.
A practical handbook for use by clergy and lay persons in ministering to the seriously ill and their families. The authors combine theory with illustrative material. It is a non-technical guide, including a listing of resources for use in the church's educational program.

Eickhoff, T.C., et. al. "A Hospitalwide Approach to AIDS." *Infection Control*, Vol. 5, No. 5, 1984, p. 243.

Fischl, M.A., et. al. "Evaluations of Heterosexual Partners, Children, and Household

Contacts of Adults with AIDS." *Journal of the American Medical Association*, Vol. 257, No. 5, February 6, 1981, pp. 640–644.

Friedland, G.H., et. al. "Lack of Transmission of HTLV-III/LAV Infection to Household Contacts of Patients with AIDS or AIDS-Related Complex with Oral Candidiasis."*The New England Journal of Medicine*, Vol. 314, No. 6, February 6, 1986, pp. 344–349.

Gostin, L. & Curran, W.J. (Editors) "AIDS: Science and Epidemiology," *Law, Medicine & Health Care*, Vol. 14, No. 5–6, December, 1986.

Kirkley-Best, Elizabeth, Kellener, Kenneth, *et al.* "On Stillbirth: An Open Letter to the Clergy." *Journal of Pastoral Care* Vol. XXXVI, No. 1, 1982, pp. 17–20.

Suggestions from a medical team to clergy in aiding parents through a stillbirth. Focuses on grief and aftercare as most important areas for clergy support.

Koop, C.E., "Surgeon General's Report on Acquired Immune Deficiency Syndrome." *Journal of the American Medical Association*, Vol. 256, No. 20, November 28, 1986, p. 2784.

Musto, D.F., "AIDS and Panic: Enemies Within." *The Wall Street Journal*, Tuesday, April 28, 1987, p. 34.

Oates, Wayne. *The Religious Care of the Psychiatric Patient*. Philadelphia, Pa.: Westminster Press, 1978.

Provides information on religious care for psychiatric patients, hospitalized and otherwise, including models of teamwork among medical professionals and clergy.

Oglesby, William Jr. *Referral in Pastoral Counseling*. Nashville, In.: Abingdon, 1978.

Focuses on when, how, and where to refer plus attention to special problems such as family resistance and legal ramifications.

Relman, Arnold S. "Christian Science and the Care of Children." *New England Journal of Medicine*, 309(36), Dec. 29, 1983, pp. 1639–1644.

In this feature called "Sounding Boards" Dr. Relman invites a former Christian Scientist, Rita Swan, whose son died of meningitis after being attended by a Christian Science practitioner, to argue the state's responsibility for the protection of children. Responding is Nathan A. Talbat, senior official of the Christian Science Church.

Robinson, A.B., "Deceiving Ourselves About 'Safe Sex'." *The Christian Century*, Vol. 104, No. 19, June 17–24, 1987, p. 550.

Sachtleben, Carl. "Pastoral Care in Breast Cancer Management." *Journal of Pastoral Care* Vol. XXXIII, No. 2, June 1979, pp. 104–109.

This is a basic step-by-step outline for pastor and chaplain of congregation-wide awareness of care and support for breast cancer patients.

Schiff, H.J. *The Bereaved Parent*. New York: Crown Publishers, Inc., 1977.

Along with the book by Claypool, this book can be given to parents who have lost a child. As the author states, "This book is not designed to tug at your heartstrings. It is meant to pull at your bootstraps; to draw you from the quagmire of grief into the land of the living."

Simonton, O.C., Matthews-Simonton, S., and Creighton, J.L. *Getting Well Again*. New York: Bantam Books, 1978.

The primary author is a radiation oncologist having much experience working with cancer patients. The book describes his approach to encouraging the mind-body connection in the process of healing. For a patient the material provides a self-help guide to using personal resources in combating illness.

Steinbrook, R. "Ethical Dimensions in Caring for Patients with AIDS." *Annals of Internal Medicine*, 103, 1985, pp. 787–790.

Torrey, E. Fuller. *Surviving Schizophrenia—A Family Manual*. San Francisco, Ca.:

Harper and Row, 1983.

This book is critical of standard mental health practices and professionals and offers ways for people to relate to schizophrenia in their own families.

Willis, R.W. "Some Concerns of Bereaved Parents." *The Journal of Religion and Health* Vol. 20(2), Summer 1981, pp. 133–140.

The author discusses the predominant themes raised by grieving parents which emerged during three years of providing a support group for them. The article is clearly written and easily read. Familiarity with its contents would aid a pastor to understand many of the concerns a parent feels in adjusting to the loss of a child.

Worden, N.W. *Grief Counseling and Grief Therapy.* New York: Springer Publishing Company, 1982.

The author is a psychologist who has had years of experience working with terminally ill patients and bereaved survivors. This monograph is more useful than any single volume on loss and grief. It should be familiar to pastors who seek to provide pastoral care for their grief-stricken parishioners.

Medical Ethics and the Pastor 6

Medical ethics has achieved prominence in the health care field due to concerns resulting from the increased use of technology in patient care. Medical ethics has been among the most thoughtful disciplines seeking to provide guidance for health care practitioners who, on occasion, face very complex ethical decisions. The legal system shares this burden. And while many practices will necessarily be translated into law, the pastor will find reliable help in becoming familiar with ethical issues in the health care field.

This section will provide a brief introduction to the field of medical ethics. Several resources are suggested in the annotated bibliography which would be useful in exploring this area further, particularly the book by Jonsen, Siegler, and Winslade, *Clinical Ethics*. The purpose of this section is to provide some insight into the types of situations the pastor will most often encounter. These situations include the process of a person becoming a patient, patient rights and responsibilities, guidelines for ethical decision-making, withholding or withdrawing treatment, "living wills" or advance directives, and resources available to the pastor which will assist his or her ministry.

Much of the discussion in this section on medical ethics has its foundation in the concept of "informed consent." It is a hinge around which both the legal and ethical dimensions of the patient-physician relationship are structured. The intent of this legal and ethical doctrine is that the physician provide the patient (to the best of the physician's ability to explain and the patient's ability to understand) truthful information about diagnosis, reasonable treatment alternatives (including uncertainties, risks, and benefits), and prognosis such that the patient can make an uncoerced decision.

Many of us who work in hospitals can recall when family would be told of diagnosis/prognosis and make treatment decisions which were withheld from the patient. Only rarely is it now legally permitted to not inform the patient. The physician's defense for withholding information is called "therapeutic privilege" and would be based on demonstrable evidence that the patient's reaction to the facts would jeopardize responsible decision-making. This position is not often defensible for a physician nor is it an excuse for returning to a paternalistic model.

Some physicians do not believe informed consent is really possible. The patient's inability to comprehend what the physician is saying or responses such as denial can complicate the process being successful. Although the patient's comprehension cannot be guaranteed, respect for personal autonomy requires that a responsible effort be made to inform. It is a basis for trust between patient and physician and shapes the nature of their relationship throughout the illness experience.

Becoming a Patient

The role of the pastor with the hospitalized parishioner may take several forms, including being a "priest," counselor, and administrator. On some occasions the minister may also function as a teacher who facilitates an understanding and embracing by the parishioner of the patient role. Becoming a patient is not easy, in that it requires a physical, emotional, and spiritual transition. A moratorium is declared on customary and important activities, roles, and responsibilities. This is usually done with the blessing of society, which recognizes that a shift is necessary in order to be treated and hopefully healed.

One dimension of being a patient which has undergone great change is the relationship with the physician, particularly when decisions about treatment are to be made. Many health care providers defined the "good" patient as one who was in compliance with the decisions made by the paternalistic physician. While some patients continue to rely on the paternalistic physician, an approach of collaborative decision-making between physician-patient is increasingly prevalent and argued for by medical ethicists. In fact, most hospitals and physicians are now guided by policies which are based upon the "collaboration" model. The field of medical ethics has argued for the benefit of this approach for patients, and the legal system continues to enhance and support an active role for the patient or patient proxy.

In Chapter Three I discussed the relationship between the patient's "partnership" role and the pastor's successful enactment of his/her role. The "partnership" role should not be confused with the "collaborative" model discussed here. "Partnership" implies that physician/hospital bring a team to the patient and the patient brings a group of players to the hospital/physician. These two teams interface and together they should cooperate to the greatest benefit of the patient. The "collaborative" model recognizes that physician and patient each bring expertise to their relationship, but of an unequal nature. The physician seeks ways to enhance the patient's understanding of diagnosis, etc., while the patient is responsible for communicating to the physician personal preferences in decision-making, based on the "informed consent" profile. In addition to the more familiar adjustments of "letting go," accepting help from others, etc., becoming a patient involves embracing "partnership" and "collaborative" relationships. The pastor can assist the patient to conceptualize these dimensions of the patient role and enact them, while being prepared to function as a member of the patient's team.

Patient Rights and Responsibilities

Few hospitals engage in the task of educating patients about their rights. Even fewer individuals have taken the initiative to learn of patient's rights. But upon experiencing hospitalization, questions relating to "rights and privileges" are considered even though they may not be thought of as such. This is most often expressed by the patient as "I sure wish I could ask my doctor some questions." The process of engaging in healing is facilitated when the patient has a sense of collaboration in the treatment process. Collaboration must involve the patient having trust in health care providers. It also is derived from knowledge that his or her personal wishes and preferences have gone into the shaping of each decision. The pastor who is acquainted with the principal contributions of medical ethics to the experiences of illness and hospitalization will be in a position to both educate and guide parishioners into full ownership of the patient role.

The first place to begin is to be aware that a list of "Patient Rights and Responsibilities" has been compiled by the American Hospital Association and is provided to hospitals and physicians.[1]

---

1. Joint Commission on Accreditation of Healthcare Organizations, "Accreditation Manual for Hospitals, 1987." 875 N. Michigan Ave., Chicago, Illinois 60611, pp. xi-xiv.

Examples of the document's content are:

1. Individuals shall be accorded impartial access to treatment or accommodations that are available or medically indicated...

2. The patient has the right to considerate, respectful care at all times...

3. The patient has the right, within the law, to personal and informational privacy...

4. The patient has the right to know the identity and professional status of individuals providing service... and to know which physician is primarily responsible for care.

5. The patient has the right to obtain...complete and current information concerning his diagnosis...,treatment and...prognosis. This information should be communicated in terms the patient can reasonably be expected to understand.

6. The patient has the right to reasonable, informed participation in decisions involving his health care.

7. The patient may refuse treatment to the extent permitted by law.

Other "rights" address personal safety, access to visitors, consultation, transfer to another facility, knowledge of hospital charges and rules. "Responsibilities" include the patient providing accurate information, being compliant with treatment decisions or responsible for refusal, financial obligations, etc. The pastor who has parishioners frequently hospitalized may want to become familiar with this document.

Guidelines for Ethical Decision-Making

The field of medical ethics provides a number of useful principles to guide decision-making, some of which have found their way into law, others into hospital policies as well as medical standards of practice. These principles apply to many of the decisions a patient or family will make. The pastor should be aware of many of these guides and be prepared to translate them into language which is as pastoral as it is clinical or philosophical. What are these guidelines? Perhaps they are best understood in the form of questions.

The first guideline is to ask the question, "What is the problem?" The risk in this question is that oversimplification, inaccuracies, or value laden criteria can render an answer useless. If value positions are taken, they need to be acknowledged. The usual experience of our Hospital Ethics Committee is that most of a consultation meeting is given to answering this question. Often, the first answer given is later discarded as further clarity is achieved. All of the relevant facts in a case provide the background for problem identification. Sometimes there is more than one problem and several problems may be mistaken to be one. Think for a moment of the complexities in the case of a diabetic who is known to be non-compliant in dietary management, and who now is in need of renal dialysis.

The facts to be discerned in determining the problem are:

1.   An accurate understanding of the illness, including the current status of the patient and the prognosis.

2.   The significant players, including medical staff, patient, family members, and the primary concerns of each.

3.   A resulting consensus of agreement among most of the players as to the specific problem(s).

The second question to be asked is, "Who should make the decision regarding a particular problem?" In most cases, law, hospital policy, or practice standards provide an answer. For example, when Jehovah's Witness parents wish to refuse procedures which would jeopardize the life of their child, the courts will authorize medical treatment recommended by the physician. Parents are instructed to leave the child in the hospital or arrange for transfer to another appropriate facility. If the court fears the parents will remove the child, then custody is temporarily given to Health and Rehabilitative Services.

When the patient is a competent adult, meaning s/he can appreciate the nature and consequences of a decision, then it is the patient who must make the decision. As discussed earlier, the role of the patient in decision-making is shaped by his/her concept of the patient-physician relationship. The collaborative model will inform the patient of relevant treatment alternatives, associated risks and probable outcome of each, and include the physician sharing his or her recommendation. The patient then decides. In the paternalistic model, the physician presents selected facts and uses weighted language to persuade the patient to do what the physician already has decided ought to be done.

It should be clear, however, that competency is not determined by whether or not the patient agrees with the physician. The competent patient has the right to refuse the physician's recommendation, even if refusal results in death, as long as the integrity of the medical profession is not violated, the interests of the state are not overridden, and the patient assumes responsibility for his or her actions. This is true not because the patient has a right to die. It is so because each of us has a legal "right to privacy." Any physician who treats despite a competent person's refusal is legally liable to charges of battery.

When the patient is not competent, or under the age of majority, the responsibility for decision-making may shift. If the patient had completed a "living will" while competent, in a state having such a statute, the wishes of the patient as expressed in that document would be followed as much as possible when the patient becomes incompetent. In such a case the patient can extend his or her decision-making authority and relieve others of that obligation. As will be discussed in more detail, a "living will" does not necessarily solve all problems in decision-making. Parents of a child will usually be the child's agent unless disagreement exists between parent and physician. In such cases, the courts often assume authority or delegate it, depending on their determination of whom best represents the interests of the child.

When decision-making falls to family, the legal order for decision-making in Florida is:

a. The patient's spouse or
b. A majority of the adult children who are reasonably available for consultation, or
c. The parents of the patient, or
d. The nearest living relative of the patient

Your state will probably follow a similar order, but specific determination is wise.

Unless a life threatening crisis is at hand, most physicians will not proceed with a treatment or procedure if obvious conflict exists within the family. This is usually true even when a spouse and adult children disagree, and the spouse has clear decision-making authority. At such times, the pastor is in a position to assist the family in conflict resolution. Fears, guilt, and perhaps misunderstanding can overshadow the responsibility to do what is in the best interests of the patient.

Some patients, when competent, will designate an agent or proxy other than family to be decision-maker when s/he becomes incompetent. There is some advantage to this approach, although family should be aware of this preference long before a crisis develops. When no family exists, the courts usually appoint a guardian for decision-making. At times this guardian is the attending physician, particularly among nursing home patients. It is probably more wise if someone other than the physician is appointed, particularly when a person familiar with decision-making issues discussed in this section is available. This is especially true for the nursing home patient because physicians are generally required to round on the patient only once a month. Although nurses will alert the physician of significant changes which occur between his/her monthly visits, most of us would prefer a more involved advocate when we can no longer represent self.

The third question which guides decision-making is, "What justifications are used for the decision that is made?" It is an appeal to identify principles because it is important to be able to explain with clarity "why" a particular decision was made. In one sense, a competent patient can decide among alternatives without a need to explain or justify. S/he is only to accept responsibility for the decision. Most major decisions, however, have impact for significant others and may require changes or commitments from one or more of them. For example, a terminally ill patient may decide to forego further curative efforts and seek hospice care, primarily on an outpatient basis. Most hospice programs accept patients only when there is a primary care person available to provide home care. Many times the primary care person is a family member. Arbitrary decision-making in my example would be unfortunate. It is usually more thoughtful, sensitive, and symbolic of a loving relationship for a patient to affirm relational regard by assisting significant others to understand his or her personal preferences.

Before the patient can be responsible to significant others, s/he must be informed by the physician of all risks and consequences. Although this is a duty which demands time from the physician, it is a responsibility which no other health professional can adequately discharge. In addition to personal needs to know, the necessity to be responsible to family is reason for the patient to accept time for asking questions of the physician.

In different ways from the patient, perhaps, family members have an equally important need to clearly understand the reasons for their decisions in behalf of the patient. Guilt is an all too present feeling even when much careful thought has guided actions. Part of the resolution process is being able to tell your "story," including the hard but responsible decisions which were made in caring for the loved one. If the patient survives, then explanations are equally as important. A recent case involved and elderly diabetic who expressed the wish to avoid mutilating surgery even if it meant losing life. While in a coma, the family gave permission for an amputation which did save her life, but resulted in a feeling of betrayal on the part of the patient. Thoughtful sharing from family restored relationship as she became assured that family had acted in a manner they felt was most loving, even if the patient would have decided differently. Further discussion helped the family have greater appreciation for the patient's position and resulted in a different decision on their part when a similar situation later developed. They refused permission for another surgical procedure because it would not change the underlying medical problem and, therefore, would not benefit the patient.

What are the issues which helped this family? First, there was a respect for the "autonomy" of the patient. This is the right to act in accordance with personal preferences and to have reasonable hope that loved ones will represent these preferences when decision-making becomes their responsibility. This responsibility is to act in accordance with what will most "benefit" the patient.

The concept of "benefit" or "best interests" of the patient is usually contrasted with the notion of "burden." Will the suffering caused by amputation, for example, likely be of more "benefit" or "burden" to the patient? Decisions which impose suffering may be of benefit if they significantly prolong the patient's life in a fashion which will be meaningful to the patient. Or, treatments may be wise if they will cause a change in the underlying primary disease process. Decisions to intervene are "burdensome," however, if they prolong or add to suffering, or extend the process of dying.

Clarity is useful regarding the probable impact of a decision. But the limits to clarity need acknowledgement. The best judgment that a treatment withheld will result in death, or given will result in survival, is usually different from knowing outcomes beyond the shadow of a doubt. Most health care professionals have witnessed a patient's recovery when the shared consensus indicated death was imminent. Nor has there necessarily been a similar pattern to these miraculous cases. In some, everything available was done for the patient. In others, decisions were made to not intervene. The pastor should be prepared to bless the family and hospital staff who must make difficult decisions when knowledge is incomplete. And remind them, despite myths of modern medicine being a pure science, that everyone stands with at least one foot on the edge of faith. Together, the patient, family, hospital staff, and pastor glimpse the mysteries of existence where no complete answers are available. The challenge is to live into the face of mystery and not be completely overcome by fear and inadequacy. In that moment we need a faith that will get us through and, in time, return us to more familiar activities, even joyous moments, enriched by the awe-filled memory of having been able to walk and not faint.

"Burden" issues which relate to costs of care are easily dealt with on the micro or local hospital level. They are more appropriately macro or national policy issues. And, as mentioned in the first chapter of this book, a lively debate is now underway regarding allocation of resources. Nevertheless, it would not be unusual for a patient and/or family to express concern. A single day in an intensive care unit, including hospital and professional costs, could devour $2500 dollars, or more. Costs escalate when physicians practice defensive medicine to avoid threats of litigation or when patients/families successfully insist on all possible intervention being employed, regardless of their appropriateness. Clarity in decision-making, on the part of all involved, will mark the largest step in the direction of cost containment while preserving quality care standards.

A few decisions will offer a unique set of circumstances which should be mentioned. The outstanding feature of this type of decision is that two very different outcomes may result. One outcome is desirable and the second outcome not desirable. However, the two outcomes are potentially inseparable. For example, a patient who is terminally ill and in much pain may require large doses of morphine in order to be made comfortable. The necessary dosage of morphine, however, may contribute to breathing difficulties to the extent that the patient might die. The pastor's guidance can assist family in understanding that the *intended* result is the desirable outcome of removing the patient's suffering. The *unintended* but unavoidable risk is that the patient will die as a result of being made comfortable. The gifts of comfort and peace usually outweigh the risks in this type of decision.

These are complicated issues. Focusing the questions of problem identification, authority, and justifications should assist decision-making. The hope is that the pastor will be a contributor to achieving clarity, so that any lasting sense of abandonment, isolation, or fracture in personal and professional relatedness is avoided. When successful, a memory of fidelity emerges as the predominant experience between the hospital/physician team and the patient's team, all of whom have contributed to decision-making.

Withholding or Another arena where pastors should have some
Withdrawing familiarity has to do with decisions where treatment
Treatment might be withheld or withdrawn. The advancement
of technology used in patient care has largely been
a blessing. A patient unfamiliar to the physician, brought to hospital
comatose with difficulty breathing, can be placed on a respirator
while it is discovered that the crisis is being caused by a drug overdose. Technology in this example usually provides time to accurately
diagnose a transient and treatable malady.

On other occasions technology has resulted in the interventions of health professionals becoming meaningless. This is
especially true when the use of technology has not supported purposeful living, but has prolonged suffering and dying. Obviously
the intent of health care professionals is to benefit the patient and
not do harm. Much of the technology we have available today
developed faster than our thoughtfulness regarding the approp-
riateness of its use.

The unfortunate cases where dying has been prolonged
usually result from a variety of influences. We have identified the
need that appropriate usage catch up with technology development.
Other factors also contribute to the confusion. Physicians are part-
ly responsible. Fear of litigation has often resulted in the practice
of defensive medicine. Many physicians have genuinely believed that
responsible behavior required the use and continuation of any
available intervention. In serious illnesses both patients and physicians are increasingly unknown to one another because referral to
a specialist and/or medical center usually results. Combine this
absence of familiarity with the average physician's discomfort in inquiring and patient preferences frequently go unclarified. With some
degree of validity, physicians will decry the litigious fires burning
in our culture and the specific attorneys who fuel it. Attorneys will
lament the malpractice which occurs and a medical profession that
inadequately disciplines its constituents.

Families also contribute. Love is confused by fear and
guilt may result in irrational insistence that hospital staff continue
all efforts. The notion of brain death is hard to understand when
the heart is visibly beating. Although it is not often discussed I have
witnessed continuation of meaningless treatment more times as a
result of family influence than because of the physician insistence.
All health care professionals have known death to be prolonged for
several days for the purpose of providing family time to adjust and
accept the loss.

But the patient or health care consumer is also to blame.
Most harbor unreal expectations of modern medicine and exalt physi-

cians to superhuman status. They do not assume a "partnership" and "collaborative" role in decisions about their health care. Nor do they necessarily communicate any better than physicians. Both patient and physician must work together to bring about changes each would prefer. The arena where this issue is most acutely focused is the situation in which the patient is believed to be hopelessly ill and decisions are appropriate for ceasing efforts to cure or manage an illness. The pastor can watch for appropriate occasions to challenge the myths and destructive behaviors of his or her parishioners.

It is also paramount that parameters be understood which influence the withholding or withdrawal decisions. Medical ethicists seem to largely agree on the following positions:

1. There is no clear moral distinction between "acting" vs. "omitting to act." The facts which permit withholding also allow for withdrawing treatment.

2. There are circumstances in which starting treatment is worse than withdrawing care. Such a case is when beginning treatment would offer a known false hope, and creates more false hopes that further things can be done.

3. Withholding/withdrawing of treatment need not get confused with abandonment of care. Treatments can be initiated with the understanding that they will be discontinued if certain goals aren't realized. It can be explained that care will always be given.

4. "Once having begun — must continue" ignores a possible change in circumstances such that what had once been designed to assist the patient may now, in fact, do positive harm, with little or no hope of benefit.

5. Nor should fear of difficulty in later withdrawing a treatment ever preclude the decision to begin a possibly lifesaving or health-improving intervention, especially an intervention that might provide a positive impact on the primary health problem.

6. There is no obligation to intervene when the gains are known to be short-term only and have no impact on the primary health problem. The "benefit-burden" polarity does not favor the patient at this juncture.

7. The moral distinction may actually cut in a direction opposite from the way we usually think: Greater justification might be needed for withholding treatment due to the uncertainty of benefit at the outset. The withdrawing of treatment has hindsight that, in fact, an intervention is of no benefit.

In addition to these consensus positions, I want to share several personal observations which have emerged from my experience as a chaplain:

1. Under most circumstances a physician is not obligated to provide futile treatment. Therefore, when the patient or family reply that s/he wants "everything done," the physician can clarify that this request will be honored by intervening wherever there is a reasonable hope of benefit.

2. No hospital policy or law is needed to excuse or protect a physician from not providing a treatment that is contraindicated in the first place.

3. It is not an act of malpractice for the physician to have treated a patient throughout the course of an illness, approach a terminal stage and not know of the patient's preferences regarding care. It is highly unprofessional, however, for the physician not to have made a reasonably skillful, deliberate effort to learn of the patient's preferences and, if known, have in the medical record an advance directive or notation making those preferences clear.

4. Without knowledge of the patient's preferences throughout the course of treatment, phrases such as "quality of life" or "a good death" are "junk" language. There are too many differences among people as illustrated by comparing Barney Clark, who wished to be attached to an external experimental mechanical heart, and Cardinal Spellman, who wished to be made comfortable.

5. Some myths may inappropriately guide professional behavior. This includes "death is the worst thing that can happen to a person."

6. It is very important for all the players in decision-making to distinguish doubt about the efficacy of withholding/withdrawing treatment from personal issues. Grief, guilt, a threat of professional failure or fear of a lawsuit can alter judgment. The guiding principle must be "benefit" to the patient.

The informed pastor can contribute to the goal of decisions which will honor the dignity and integrity of all persons. Critical moments will emerge when gentle and informed suggestions or questions can result in a clear focus on the issue at hand. There will be few resources, if any, other than the pastor who can assist in resolving enough of the clouds of guilt, fear, and helplessness which shroud the real issues.

Another issue receiving much recent attention will only be mentioned. It is the decision to withdraw or withhold food and water from some patients. Increasingly, decisions are being supported by the courts which involve discontinuing nutrition and/or hydration. It is an emotion-filled issue because of the symbolism as well as the harsh notions of thirst and starvation. Nursing homes more so than hospitals will probably become the primary setting for these types of decisions. The pastor who has a large representation of elderly or nursing home bound members would be wise to become familiar with this particular development. In some cases, providing nutrition and hydration serves only to prolong dying. Withdrawing these supports in appropriate cases which are almost always being provided by artificial means, such as an I.V., does not make the patient uncomfortable.

In the neo-natal patient, decisions to withdraw or withhold treatment are shaped by criteria which may not include determination of brain death. Two of the necessary criteria for the diagnosis of brain death, establishing cessation of cerebral and brainstem functions, as well as confirming irreversibility, are very difficult to fulfill in the newborn and young infant,[2] particularly in cases of asphyxia. Most often, decisions to withhold or withdraw treatment are made based on "best interests" of the seriously ill infant.

A related phenomenon to the cessation of treatment decision is the question of organ or tissue donation. Increasingly states are passing laws which are referred to as "routine inquiry" or "required request." Where such laws exist hospital staff must approach family whenever the patient is dying and has been determined to be eligible for donating, including major organs such as heart or kidney, but also corneas, skin, or bone. Exceptions to this formal request are situations where the patient or family has previously indicated a clear preference as to donation. Although never an easy decision, nor a comfortable task for hospital staff to inquire, the pastor should always anticipate a request and prayerfully respond to the concerns which family express. Regardless of the fact that most clergy favor organ donation, we are in a unique position to help the family arrive at a comfortable decision, without burdening them with any bias.

I have marveled on many occasions at families who felt they created meaning out of absurdity by donating a loved one's organs, particularly when the death was the result of a sudden, unexpected event. Some families have later expressed regrets when they were not offered the alternative of donating. There may be several

---

2. Volpe, J. "Brain Death Determination in the Newborn." *Pediatrics*, Vol. 80, No. 2, August, 1987, pp. 293-297.

reasons for hospital staff not inquiring. The pastor should be prepared to explain, even at a later date, why the family was not asked about donation. Sometimes a request was not made because staff felt the family was too emotionally distraught to be approached. With "required request" statutes, however, hospitals will no longer be able to rely on their discretion. The pastor should be prepared to explain this also.

Pastors can encourage families to discuss their individual preferences regarding organ donation during times of good health. What parishioners need is good information and helpful guides to assist their thinking. All of the major religious groups support organ donation. A 1986 Gallup poll indicated that over 95% of all Americans have an awareness of transplant needs but only 50% of individuals who are members of religious groups would likely donate after their death. This percentage of willing donors is in line with a survey which involved persons who were not religious.

At the time of this writing, approximately 10,000 persons are on a waiting list for kidneys and 400 wait for hearts. One donor has the capability to save the lives of as many as seven persons and provide treatment for up to fifty others. With only 15-20% of available organs actually donated and harvested, many questions exist as to how to increase the number of donors. This is especially interesting when almost all religious groups support donation but only 50% of their members indicate a willingness to donate. How do we overcome the present limits of volunteerism?

Pastors can encourage family discussion by:

1. Educating parishioners about the current practice of transplantation, including meeting transplant recipients.

2. Making families aware that even if one member signs a donor card it will still be the family's decision regarding donation.

3. Helping individuals/families think through issues, perhaps by discussing the following questions:
   a. Who has "custody" of organs once a person is brain dead?
   b. Does an individual/family own the body or have stewardship over it?
   c. What is the relationship between personal autonomy, respect for life, and responsibility to others?
   d. Is there a relationship between the believer's role in creation and donation?
   e. Is there a reason to object to donation if one believes in a physical resurrection?

f. Does confusion exist between cultural/personal/emotional objections to donation and religious beliefs?

g. If organs/tissues, etc. are donated, can a funeral include a viewing of the body?

"Living Wills" or Advanced Directives   A "living will" or an advance directive is an increasingly important and prevalent means whereby a person can extend his or her treatment preferences if and when s/he becomes incompetent. A patient's living will or directive has no direct effect, therefore, until the patient becomes incompetent. While competent, preferences are determined by speaking with the patient. There are at least four types of directives, including a "living will," a proxy directive, the combination of a "will" and proxy, and durable power of attorney. As of this writing, thirty-eight states and the District of Columbia have advance directive statutes. Although similar in intent, each may vary somewhat and a pastor should become familiar with the law in his or her state. Where no law exists, information can be obtained by writing The Society for the Right To Die (250 West 57 Street, New York 10107).

The directive most often seen in popular literature is the "living will." Although the requirements vary from state to state, it is a document intended to allow the individual to make treatment instructions if s/he becomes hopelessly ill and incompetent. It should be completed while of sound mind, be witnessed by two persons (one of whom may not be a spouse or blood relative), and should be discussed with a personal physician and placed in the declarant's medical record. It is best to discuss the completion of this document with family and significant others. And, as a precaution it should be updated by personal signature and witnesses every few years. The "will" remains in effect until it is revoked by the initiator. If revoked, the personal physician should be informed of the change.

Benefits of having an advance directive make it desirable to recommend your parishioners seriously consider completing one. At a minimum they provide an opportunity for families to discuss personal preferences apart from a crisis. Should the situation arise, it is extremely comforting to know with certainty what a loved one prefers. It allows for individual respect and autonomy to be extended into a time when the emotional forces influencing decision-making are often not available for rational discussion. Family members can be relieved of burdensome responsibilities. To some extent, so can physicians. It is a way for the patient to have thoughtfully prepared loved ones for a time which is difficult at best.

Problems with the "living will" are potentially significant. The state in which you reside may not have a statute and a "will" would have moral import only. Some argue that a "will" is not needed anyway if patient and physician have communicated ahead of time. Unfortunately the literature is filled with reports of difficulty with communication. Another problem is that a physician other than the familiar family practitioner may be attending during a serious illness. Some mechanism for dealing with this potential development must be prearranged. A third problem is that a "will" cannot account for every potential circumstance during the course of a terminal phase. For example, what if the patient develops a pneumothorax, which is a reversible malady. Should the family give permission when the physician offers the treatment alternative? Yet another problem is that language is often vague. Many "wills" speak of avoiding "extraordinary means." How does one always know what is "extraordinary"? Parishioners should be encouraged to be as specific as possible and to seek guidance from their physician about wording in the living will. Most "wills" require the patient to be terminally ill. What about when the patient is in a permanent vegetative state, but not terminally ill? Slowly the courts are clarifying this requirement. Some persons specify particular interventions they wish withheld, such as I.V. nutrition. Possible physician or hospital challenge to these exceptions could result in lengthy court battles, while the patient is maintained by support contrary to original preference. As more of these types of cases are settled through the courts issues will be clarified.

There is also opposition based on values. Some have argued that allowing persons to refuse treatment violates the sanctity of life and represents a step toward the "slippery slope" which leads to active euthanasia. Others have expressed a concern that autonomy and personal identity could undergo undetected changes. That is, the person who originally signed the "will" may not be the same person who is ill and incompetent. A final objection has been a concern about legal minimalism. Some believe that the least law is the best, particularly laws which interfere with the patient-physician relationship and run the risk of making it more adversarial.

A second type of directive is for the individual to appoint a proxy decision-maker. This is usually a family member but may be anyone the patient chooses. It must be a person who understands the preferences of the patient and makes decisions based on those preferences. Such a designee avoids the problem of confusing language in a "will." If a proxy is used, the patient should select a person respected by family and thoughtfully inform family of the selection. An acceptable proxy can relieve family members of decision-making burdens.

A third directive is the combination of a "will" and proxy. This approach would combine the strengths of each while overcoming most of the weaknesses in a "will" by the presence of a proxy. The proxy in this case makes treatment decisions not specifically focused by the patient's living will. The fourth alternative is the best known proxy directive, durable power of attorney. This is a court-appointed person who becomes the "guardian of decision-making." It has many of the advantages of the proxy directive, and may best serve a nursing home population who are often underrepresented. Problems relate to the cumbersome process of court proceedings and the important question, "What is the proxy's responsibility when the patient is competent?"

Advance directives have come into existence because of the possibility that dying could be prolonged. They relate to the primary values of preserving and extending personal autonomy, of individual liberty, and rights to privacy. They have the potential of providing relief to patients, families and physicians, particularly when strife or conflict exists. If the patient prefers to avoid aggressive interventions when conditions are believed hopeless, directives should contribute to lower health care costs, which will benefit society as a whole.

The success of advance directives requires the pastor to educate his or her parishioner during times free of illness. Reports of cases where a "living will" is brought by family to a physician, during a crisis, where the patient is not known to the physician will usually result in extended delays before the directive is honored, if at all.[3] Hospitals must be certain that relatives do not have a vested interest in the demise of the patient. Preparation and communication among patient, family and physician ahead of time is crucial to the functional value of any directive. One of our physicians expressed this concern by saying, "I want my patient to say to me, 'Doc, I enjoy my life and want to live meaningfully as long as possible. But when I become ill and there is no hope for my recovery, then I do not want you to do anything that will prolong my dying or the suffering of my loved ones. Just make me as comfortable as you can.' "

---

3. *Law, Medicine & Health Care*, Vol. 13, No. 6, December, 1985, pp. 260–282.

Resources for   Useful resources may be available to the pastor who
the Pastor   would benefit from thinking through these issues
prior to providing guidance to the family. More than
half of the hospitals in the United States now have bioethics committees. These committees are composed of an interdisciplinary group
of health professionals who have familiarized themselves with ethical
issues as they relate to patient care decisions. Many of these committees are consulted regularly by physicians or other staff when
complex issues emerge. Most committees include physicians, nurses,
social workers, clergy, administrators, ethicists, and lay persons.
Although the pastor does not need to consult with the entire committee, a call to the chairperson of the committee could result in an
opportunity to talk with one member.

A word of caution, however. These ethics committees
are relatively new developments in hospitals. With few exceptions
most are building trust and rapport with hospital staff so they
will be viewed as a positive advisory and consultative resource,
and not be seen as a threat to usurp the sanctity of the physician-
patient relationship. Consequently the best approach for a pastor is to take the initiative to meet members of the committee
during non-crisis times so that a communication link is established for possible future use. When this preparation has not
occurred, an inquiry through the hospital director or chief of
staff's office, which makes clear the pastor's need, will usually
facilitate contact with the chairperson. An equally useful resource
is the hospital chaplain who is frequently conversant with medical
ethics issues and may serve on the committee. Reading material
is referenced at the end of this section.

Bibliography

Annas, G. "Transferring the Ethical Hot Potato." *The Hastings Center Report*,
February, 1987, pp. 20–21.
This article provides an insightful discussion of four patient cases (Bartling, Bouvia,
Requena and Brophy) where hospitals sought to transfer the patient or impose
treatment alternatives different from patient preferences. Each patient was
competent to make treatment choices different from those recommended by
the medical personnel.

Cranford, R.E., and Doudera, A.E. (Eds.) *Institutional Ethics Committees and Health
Care Decision Making.* Ann Arbor, Michigan: Health Administration Press,
1984.
Ron Cranford is a neurologist at Hennepin County Medical Center in Minneapolis,
Minnesota. Edward Doudera is Executive Director of the American Society of

Law and Medicine. Cranford has as much practical experience as anyone with I.E.C. and Doudera's organization has sponsored the most thoughtful educational conference about such committiees. The book is an excellent resource for learning about the function, purpose, and limitations of hospital ethics committees.

Eisendrath, S. and Jonsen, A. "The Living Will." *Journal of the American Medical Association,* 249 (15), 1983, pp. 34–38.
This article provides a helpful discussion of the "living will" and the help it provides as well as the issues it leaves to be resolved.

Gorovitz, S., et. al. (Eds) *Moral Problems in Medicine.* Englewood Cliffs, New Jersey: Prentice-Hall, Inc. 1976.
This book can serve as a textbook for the pastor who discovers a keen interest in medical ethics.

Hastings Center Report. Hastings-on-Hudson, New York 10706–9985. Institute of Society, Ethics, and the Life Sciences.
Although the number of periodicals focusing on medical ethics has increased during recent years, the Hastings Center continues to produce a quality report. If the pastor's budget permits subscription to journals in specialized fields, this report will be a resource which will routinely update the reader.

Jonsen, A.J., Siegler, M., and Winslade, W.J. *Clinical Ethics.* New book: Macmillan Publishing Co., Inc., 1982.
If the pastor is going to have one book as a resource, this is the one to purchase. It is very complete for such a small volume and has a clinical orientation, which makes it more practical. Although written primarily for physicians and health professionals, most pastors will find it helpful.

Lynn, J. and Childress, J. "Must Patients Always be Given Food and Water?" *Hastings Center Report,* Vol. 13, October, 1983, pp. 17–21.
Other articles exist, but this remains the best simple reading on the subject. Joanne Lynn has a great deal of practical experience as a physician working with nursing home and hospice patients.

Rachals, J. *The End of Life.* New York: Oxford University Press, 1986.
Rachals is a philosopher who writes well. His book deals with the thorny topic of euthanasia, highlighting eastern and western traditions while suggesting a solution which goes beyond each. There is every indication that active voluntary euthanasia will become a focus of debate in the coming decade. For that reason, this book is helpful in clearly addressing these issues.

Selected reports of the President's Commission for the Study of Ethical Problems in Medicine and Biomedical and Behavioral Research: *Deciding to Forego Life-Sustaining Treatment; Defining Death; Making Health Care Decisions.* Washington, D.C. Government Printing Office, 1981–83.
The three separate volumes mentioned above in the President's Commission series would be wise additions to a church library or the pastor's study. Along with the book by Jonsen, and the *Hasting's Center Report,* the minister library on medical ethics would rate an A+ when compared to that of most.

Veatch, R.M. *Case Studies in Medical Ethics.* Cambridge, Massachusetts: Harvard University Press, 1977.
Professor Veatch's book is an excellent companion to the Gorovitz book mentioned earlier. A variety of complex medical cases are provided to illustrate identifying ethical issues and then exploring the question, "What is the right thing to do?"

Wanzer, S.H., et. al. "The Physician's Responsibility Toward Hopelessly Ill Patients." *New England Journal of Medicine,* 310:15, April 12, 1984, pp. 955–959.

This article presents a thoughtful model for levels of medical intervention based upon the condition of a patient who is terminally ill. It can be used as a guide for discussion in any educational efforts the pastor might structure for parishioners. Physicians would both contribute and benefit from participation in these educational efforts, as a number of questions would emerge which are best handled by an M.D.

Training Lay Caregivers in Hospital Visitation 7

When I asked different clergy about programs for training lay hospital visitors in their congregations, my favorite response came from my colleage Rabbi Allan Lehmann. He did not have such a program in his congregation but a friend of his did. "He calls them 'Rabbinic Para-Professionals,'" said Rabbi Lehmann. "We just used to call them Jews!"

Of course that is true in the Church as well. We can develop all sorts of titles, descriptions and training programs for people who visit other church people in the hospital, but it could also be said that once we just called these people Christians. It is important to remember that the visiting of the sick is a ministry of the whole Church. In part, this chapter will deal with ways to enable all church members to be part of this ministry. It is also true that certain tasks require specific skills and training. We will discuss the ways and means of this training.

Many books on lay caregiving begin with involved justifications of why the laity should be involved in what is otherwise known as "Pastoral Care." Lengthy rationales are used to break down the resistance of pastor and congregation to the notion of shared ministry. Let us accept here that churches do understand that the visitation of the hospitalized is a realm of ministry which all share. Given that understanding, we will offer a variety of ways to organize, resource, and support lay hospital visitors in the church.

I have three assumptions. First, no matter what size the church, the pastor can always use assistance in hospital visitation. Second, hospital patients can always benefit from the care of people other than the pastor. Third, members of the congregation benefit from opportunities for significant Christian service to their sisters and brothers in this special time of need.

I will present three models for involving church members in hospital visiting. Model 1 is informal resourcing. In this the pastor enables church members to understand their own opportunities for hospital visitation as these situations arise. Model 2 is recruitment and network building. Here the pastor recruits individuals for hospital visiting to supplement the pastor's calls, and networks of congregational support are developed. Model 3 is training lay caregiving teams. Here special teams of lay caregivers are organized and given extensive training for hospital visitation.

Implicit in our understanding of all these programs for training and resourcing lay visitors is a commitment to continued pastoral supervision of the lay visitor. That supervision may be as simple as a phone call to a friendly visitor in the first model for small churches, a follow up session with the visitor in Model 2, or regular case conferences with the visitor in the formal program of Model 3. Hospital visitation always involves ongoing sensitivity to issues of confidentiality, spiritual direction, physical well-being, and connection to the church community. Good supervision involves a give-and-take on these issues between pastor and visitor. The lay visitor's work is a complement to and not a substitute for the pastor's care of the hospital patient.

Model 1— Informal Resourcing
The first model is an enabling style. It is best suited for the small church, but should be part of the resourcing of visitors for all churches. For example, church member Fred greets Pastor Judy Davis on Sunday morning and tells her that church member George went into the hospital for tests yesterday. Typically, Pastor Davis could hear this as a criticism ("Why didn't you know this already?"), or a challenge ("Why didn't you see him already?"). Model 1 sees this as an opportunity for resourcing and enabling a new hospital visitor. Pastor Davis, instead of saying, "Yes, I saw him yesterday," or "I will see him this afternoon," which relieves Fred of any further involvement, could begin by finding out more about Fred's support for George in the hospital. How did Fred hear about George? Has Fred visited George? If so, then Pastor Davis would interpret this visit as good pastoral care, part of the church's ministry. Fred has already begun his role as hospital

visitor and Pastor Davis can now enable Fred's continuation in this role. It would be appropriate to take some time right here if possible or set an appointment to explore what kind of visitation Fred might continue for George.

This is how model 1 begins, by enabling and re-sourcing the people who are already involved with the patient in some way. The pastor then contacts the patient to find out other people in his or her support group who would be good visitors. Other questions are then asked both of the patient and those who visit. Are there needs in the patient's home which church members can look after? What kind of help and information regarding the hospital visiting would be useful to the visitor at this time?

By now Fred is part of the care team that is developing for George. Pastor Davis has gently begun to structure an informal network of lay visitation that was already latent in the church. While churches of all sizes can facilitate this kind of informal caregiving, this style of enabling is especially well suited for the small church.

Most systems of lay caregiving are designed for large churches. They involve recruitment, training, and committee structuring, which are good for large churches but overwhelming for the small church. The small church functions well along friendship and kinship lines. This is why it is important to nurture and support the existing if unidentified framework for care and visitation which already exists in the small church.

Members of small churches often have difficulty seeing that their individual hospital calls and visits are part of a wholistic scheme of pastoral care which is shared with the ordained minister. The goal of the pastor in model 1 is to identify, support, and make visible the value of hospital visitation which individual members undertake. The pastor then gives those who are already visiting the skills and resources to make them even better visitors. The pastor should always interpret to visitor, patient, and congregation that such visitation is a ministry of the church shared by pastor and congregation.

That raises the question of training. The small church does not need to engage in the long-term systematic education program for hospital visitation required in the large church. Training in model 1 can be done in two ways. First, it is worthwhile to spend individual time with people who emerge as good visitors. Go over the guidelines of this book with them. Help them understand that the gift they offer is a supportive, listening presence. They are not supposed to solve all the problems of the patients they visit. Remind the visitor of the issues of confidentiality.

Let the visitor know that a short prayer signifies to both patient and visitor that they are not alone in this illness. Listen to the visitor express both gifts and concerns. Accept the concerns and encourage the visitor in the sharing of those gifts.

A second form of training which is practical in the small church is the sermon. First of all, a sermon can remind the congregation that lay visitation is complementary to the pastor's visits. Celebrate this shared ministry in a time when people in the church are visiting a hospitalized church member. This visitation can be used as an example of shared ministry. Supporting what is being done is preferable to a harangue over what should be done.

Secondly, the sermon can be an occasion to share the guidelines of good hospital visitation. When one person in a small church is hospitalized, it may affect the whole congregation. An event such as this in the life of the congregation can become a time for both nurture and learning. Issues of hospital visitation can be discussed on a regular basis connecting the biblical themes of healing and visiting the sick with the life of the congregation.

In most small churches, and most Protestant churches in America are small churches, the enabling style of model 1 is all that is needed in the training of lay hospital visitors. Perhaps the critical issue of model 1 and the small church is enabling lay visitors to understand the limits of their intervention. Develop clear and attainable goals for visitation with the visitor. These should include limits on the number and length of visits. The pastor may need to monitor length and frequency of visits and help the visitor make any adjustments according to the patient's needs.

One of the beautiful parts of belonging to a small church is that when you are sick, you can count on lots of good care from pastor and congregation. The informal resourcing style of model 1 makes sure this will happen.

Model 2 — Recruiting and Networking   While informal resourcing of model 1 can and should continue in the middle size church, here it becomes necessary to organize for hospital visitation. The middle size church, with 100-250 people in attendance on a Sunday morning, is too large for informal visitation by pastor or congregation. A system needs to be developed for identifying those in need of hospital visits and those who will do the visiting.

The middle size church only needs a few people who are willing to do hospital visiting. They may be part of a standing committee or organized just for this purpose. Each church and community is different. A younger congregation will need fewer visitors than one with older members. The location and number of hospitals in the area will also make a difference as to how many visitors it will take to cover the responsibility. Each church should determine the extent of its needs for lay visitors.

Even though the number of visitors is small, it should be diverse, including men and women, young and old. Persons who exhibit skills in listening and interest in caring for people who are ill should be invited to consider this role of hospital visitor. The pastor should offer one or two training sessions and then continue with regular support for these volunteers once they have begun their visits. It is important to gather this small team of visitors regularly so that they feel encouragement from the pastor and each other.

In the medium size church, everyone does not know each other, so the pastor should determine from the patient first if s/he is comfortable with one of the church members coming to visit. The visitor should always be clear that she or he is visiting on behalf of the church and ask the patient if a return visit would be welcome.

The feelings of the patient, not the visitor, are primary here, and the pastor may have to help the church visitor understand this. The authority to enter a hospital room comes from the patient. Ministers generally have this permission because of their relationship. Church visitors need to ask if this authority is extended to them.

The pastor should introduce these recruited lay visitors to key hospital personnel, especially the chaplain or social worker if there is one. Time should be taken for the visitor to talk with these hospital professionals to give the visitor personal perspectives on hospital visitation.

A second tier of hospital care is thus added in the medium size church. The position of hospital visitor is perhaps most crucial in the medium size church, because this church is typically understaffed. In fact many medium size churches find that recruiting, training, hiring, and even paying lay church people on a part time basis to share tasks such as hospital visiting is an excellent way to make sure this vital element of the church's ministry is covered.

Once hospital visitors are recruited and trained, however, the model 1 approach must not be forgotten. The difference here is that the medium size church has numerous subgroups from which the informal visitors can come.

Besides the identified hospital visitors, the pastor should also identify the people in the church who are the informal support system for the hospital patient and make them part of the hospital visitation team. Again, their role is more limited than either the pastor or the trained hospital visitor, but they should be given skills for good hospital visiting as well.

Some medium size churches find it sufficient to use the existing networks as support systems for times such as this. Boards, study groups, fellowship groups, Sunday School classes are all logical to consider as support systems for a hospitalized church member. Other medium size churches develop intentional networks of support for people in any time of crisis. These can be done geographically, by interest, or by commitment. A medium size church is well suited to have church-wide networks which include everyone in some way. There is often resistance to such structure, for it symbolizes some loss of the intimacy which had been experienced when this was a single cell church. But it is worth exploring ways that the medium size church can develop systems or networks of support that include everyone.

By its very nature, the medium size church is in transition. Its system for hospital visitation will probably have to be revised regularly as size and circumstance change. As described here it is a hybrid between the small and large church visiting model. Again, the key word may be accepting limitation. Do not overload the medium size church with a training system for visitation that it neither wants nor needs. Also remind the visitors again of their limitations. A visit is just that, not a therapy session or a time for miracles.

Model 3— Trained Lay Caregiving Teams

In a large church, hospital visiting must be done systematically. Often one member of a multiple staff takes key responsibility for this task, but it is never enough for this staff member to do all hospital visiting alone. As mentioned earlier, both congregation and patient benefit by the giving and receiving of extended care by lay visitors.

Here the key is teamwork. A team of lay visitors need to be trained and recruited at regular intervals. Visitation may be the responsibility of a formal board, part of the church structure, chaired by one of the team members. It is important that this team meet regularly for sharing and support, for their work can become difficult and lonely.

In the large church, where it is often the case that visitor and patient will not know each other personally, training becomes most important. Good intentions are not enough, and a visitor can do more harm than good.

Begin by making the plan for hospital visitation public, let people volunteer, but also recruit people who are well suited to this task. The initial meeting should be open and informational. The goals, level of commitment, and training should be made very clear. Then individuals should be given a chance to decide if they wish to commit to this responsibility.

Many programs of lay caregiving require an individual interview with each prospective lay visitor. Many potential visitors self-select out of the process at this point because of the commitment required. But there are times when people who should not do hospital visiting do come for an interview. This is an important time to screen out anyone who would not be helpful as a hospital visitor.

This stage becomes very delicate and important. Lay visitors should have a certain maturity. They should be people who represent the church well and be stable in their own lives. They must be good listeners and have the ability to put aside their own needs in order to focus on the needs of the patient. They must also exhibit an understanding of confidentiality.

The prospect of rejecting a church volunteer strikes fear in the heart of most pastors (at least it does mine!), so here are some guidelines for softening that blow, if it should become necessary. First, the interview for hospital visitation should include filling out a form which includes other interests as well. Then if the candidate would not be suitable for hospital visiting, he or she could be rerouted to another area of service in which he or she has already expressed interest. Secondly, the interview can be carried out by a steering committee. Then if a candidate is rejected, the hostility may not be directed at the pastor (completely). Third, this kind of caregiving often attracts people who are under significant stress in their own lives. The person's interest can be gently interpreted as a request for help and the appropriate referral made. The pastor can stay in touch with this person and if interest remains, then at a later time they can be involved in the training program.

It may be necessary to turn some people down. It is also important to realize that no matter how well you do this, these people may well be angry at the church for doing this. But remember, this is a time when the primary concern must be for the patient, not the visitor.

Once a team of lay caregivers is screened and recruited, then a schedule for training should be developed. Clear commitments to follow through the training should be made. Consider the characteristics of your group and determine the best training schedule for these people. Often a weekend retreat is a good way to start. This should be followed by a series of weekly meetings.

Here are some guidelines for training.

1. Begin with good group process techniques. Take time to let people share who they are and build group trust. Spiritual grounding should be part of this and every meeting. Use I Corinthians 12, or Romans 12, to enable people to identify the gifts which have called them to this place. Gordon Cosby, of the Church of Our Savior in Washington, D.C., emphasizes that it is important for everyone to begin by understanding our gifts as that which brings joy and energy. Our gifts are the essence of who we are. When we live our gifts, we have the time of our lives, and in this place we call forth the depth of gifts in each other.[1] Take time to let each person share the gifts they perceive in themselves. Let the group affirm one another's gifts.

2. Session two should begin with time for spiritual centering, and personal sharing. This should remain a part of every session, reinforcing the notion that the group will be a place individuals receive support as they go out to support others. Then begin with presentation of data on hospital visitation. We recommend following the outline of information in this book. If possible, invite a hospital chaplain or social worker to introduce current issues in health care and visitation.

3. As you go through the information presented in this book, take time to deal with relevant areas experientially. For example, let people share their own good and bad experiences of being visited by clergy, friends, and well-meaning church people when they were either in the hospital or part of a family in a crisis situation. Share the guided meditation on wholistic healing with the group and discuss responses. Take a session to explore the theology of prayer. In dealing with the chapters on the child as patient, and the terminal patient, do some role playing.

4. Keep returning to the issues of confidentiality, listening, and the limitation of expectations.

5. Make the transition from training to visiting. With this much training, more than the average level of anxiety may arise about visiting the first patient. Leadership

---

1. E. O'Connor, *Journey Inward, Journey Outward*, New York: Harper & Row, 1975 p. 37.

should be sensitive to this and assist the visitor in the first visit, following up then with questions and support for subsequent visits.

6. Establish regular gathering times for the sharing of experiences and continued support for the group.

This is a brief outline of a sample training program. It is easy to turn all attention away from the congregation as a whole when such an intensive training program as this is underway. Remember, then, that this group can also facilitate the informal care networks of models 1 and 2 among other members of the congregation.

Remember to interpret the role of lay caregiving to the congregation. Newsletter articles, informational flyers, and announcements during worship are all important in keeping the congregation informed about this style of caregiving. Always remind the congregation that this is part of the partnership of ministry, not the stronghold of a selected few.

This then is the overview of training lay caregivers for hospital visitation. Each church is unique with special circumstances determining the best way to carry out the visitation of hospital patients. Always examine your own situation first and develop a program which suits the particular needs of your congregation and community.

Bibliography

Barr, Browne and Eakin, Mary. *The Ministering Congregation.* New York: Pilgrim Press, 1972.
This book provides a structure for the kind of mission a congregation can develop which leads to a broad sense of community and responsibility. From this context, Browne Barr's churches have developed lay caregiving ministries.

Detwiler-Zapp, Diane, and Dixon, William Caveness. *Lay Caregiving.* Philadelphia: Fortress Press, 1982.
A step by step outline for developing lay teams for pastoral care in the local congregation.

Haugk, Kenneth, "The Stephen Series," a special training program in lay caregiving.
This is a specific program in lay caregiving headquartered at 7120 Lindell Blvd., St. Louis, Missouri 63130. It contains a format for extensive training of clergy and laity for pastoral care, including hospital visitation.

Saylor, Dennis. *A Guide to Hospital.* Baker Book House, 1984.
A guide for lay church visitors in hospital calling.

Stone, Howard W. *The Caring Church.* San Francisco: Harper and Row, 1983.
An outline for a congregational training program in pastoral care, including hospital visitation.

Glossary of Medical Terms
Charles A. Williams, M.D.

As you make your hospital rounds, a particular parishioner requests communion prior to having surgery. Out of the corner of your eye you notice a prominently placed sign above her bed with the abbreviation "NPO." It is helpful to know she can have "nothing by mouth." Instead of being caught off guard and proceeding with communion, which might cause a postponement of surgery, knowledge of what NPO means enables you to remind her of the restriction while carefully responding to her request for spiritual comfort, prayer, and assurance of God's presence.

There are many terms commonly used in hospitals which would be helpful to know. This chapter contains a glossary of such terms but it is not meant to substitute for a medical dictionary. Nor does it give complete explanations since there are too many exceptions and complexities in medicine to allow such completeness. For accurate information about a disease in an individual, the best resource is the patient's physician.

Another important source of hospital information is the medical record department. Hospitals are required, under most state licensing laws, to have an updated list of accepted and approved abbreviations that may be used in the medical records. Most medical record departments would gladly provide you with such a list and this list may be of help in de-coding some medical terminology abbreviations.

Aneurysm balloon-like dilation of an artery. It may occur in any artery of the body but commonly occurs in arteries of the brain or in the aortic artery.

Angina a severe, constricting pain. Angina usually means pain that originates from or is associated with decreased blood supply to the heart muscle.

Anomaly anything that is unusual or not normal; commonly used in reference to a congenital birth defect. For example, abnormal development of a valve inside the heart might be referred to as a cardiac valve anomaly.

Aphasia the condition of a loss of neurological ability resulting from an injury or disease involving a critical area of brain functioning or processing. Speech, language, writing and other selective, receptive or expressive skills may be impaired or absent in aphasia disorders.

Arrhythmia abnormal heart beat. Some arrhythmias can be life threatening; most are incidental and cause no difficulty.

Arteriogram (angiogram) an x-ray picture outlining the blood flow through an artery. The picture is obtained by performing an x-ray while an artery is injected with a liquid that will be detected by the x-ray. The same process can be used in veins and that is called a venogram.

Ascites an accumulation of fluid inside the abdominal cavity. This usually is associated with liver failure or kidney failure.

Attending Physician the primary physician in charge of or responsible for the overall medical care of the patient. This physician usually writes all medical orders and approves and directs the evaluation and treatment of the patient. To be distinguished from a consultative physician and a physician in training such as an intern, resident, or fellow.

Barium enema an x-ray examination of the lower intestine, especially the rectum and colon, which uses a liquid material (barium) that is detected by the x-ray. The liquid is given by an enema and the inside of the intestine is thus outlined and photographed.

Benign refers to the mild nature of an illness or, when referring to tissue growth, means that the tissue is not malignant (or cancerous).

Bilirubin a red pigment which is found in bile. Bilirubin is derived from the hemoglobin in red blood cells. It is concentrated by the liver and excreted in the form of bile. Excess accumulation of this pigment in the blood causes jaundice or yellow skin and is commonly due to liver injury or to blood diseases which cause rapid destruction of red blood cells. A mild form of jaundice, however, can be present in newborn infants and is a normal developmental event.

Biopsy the removal and examination of a piece of body tissue for diagnosis. Usually, the biopsy specimen is obtained by an incision or by skin puncture with a specifically designed needle.

Brain death a term that is used to describe a state of apparent life in which the body is living but the brain is dead. Many states and most hospitals have precise definitions of brain death that usually involve the criteria of absent electrical activity on repeated electroencephalograms (a "flat" EEG) and the physical absence of primitive nerve reflexes.

Bypass refers to an operation which shunts blood from one area to another. Often performed to bypass an obstructed or occluded artery in the heart (aorto-coronary bypass).

Carcinoma — a tumor which is cancerous. Carcinomas can often be identified as arising from a specific tissue such as breast, liver, lung, or muscle. When no specific tissue of origin can be identified, the term undifferentiated carcinoma is used.

Cardiac arrest — an emergency situation in which the heart stops beating.

Cardiopulmonary arrest — an emergency situation in which the heart stops beating and the lungs stop breathing concurrently.

Catheterization — the process of sliding a catheter into a lumen of the body. Lumens may include an artery, vein, urethra, etc. Catheters are small tubes which are passed into the lumen. Catheterization often refers to cardiac catheterization in which a catheter is placed through an artery or vein and into the heart. A liquid which can be detected by x-ray is then injected and x-ray pictures can be taken which outline the interior chambers and valves.

CAT Scan (CT scan) — computerized axial tomogram scan. A process whereby multiple x-rays of the body are integrated using a computer so that a picture is developed which illustrates the internal anatomy. The test was first developed for use in studying the brain but this type of scanning is now applicable to all parts of the body.

Chemotherapy — treatment of disease by chemicals. These chemicals often interfere with cell growth or kill certain cells. Undesired damage to healthy cells may ensue and is termed "toxicity." This therapy is often used for the treatment of malignant diseases but can also be used for other severe diseases of unknown cause.

Colostomy — a surgical procedure which establishes an artificial opening by connecting the colon to the abdominal wall surface. It allows fecal contents to exit through the opening in the abdominal wall without requiring its passage through the normal rectum and anus. May be a temporary or permanent procedure.

Coma a state of unconsciousness from which the person cannot be awakened. There are many causes which include chemical abnormalities in the blood, brain trauma, cerebral hemorrhage and tumors.

Cystoscopy see *oscopy*

Death see *brain death*

Diabetes refers to a medical condition characterized by an excessive discharge of urine. It may occur when blood sugar is elevated as in diabetes mellitus. Diabetes insipidus refers to an increased amount of urine which may be due to tremendous water ingestion unassociated with increased blood sugar.

Dialysis the process of purifying blood by filtering out abnormal chemicals which would otherwise be removed by the kidneys. Prolonged, severe kidney failure may require blood dialysis (hemodialysis) in order to eliminate toxic agents. This requires that blood be circulated outside the body, by use of special catheters and filtration machines. The purified blood is then "transfused" back into the blood stream. The blood is withdrawn and returned through veins, or surgically constructed arterio-venous shunts, in the arm or leg. Peritoneal dialysis refers to a dialysis method that does not involve direct cleansing of blood but involves cleansing of abdominal fluid (peritoneal fluid) by instilling and withdrawing fluid from the abdomen. The exchanges occur by use of a peritoneal catheter that is punctured or surgically inserted into the abdomen.

Do not resus— citate (DNR) Usually a physician order, written in the patient's medical record, indicating that certain life sustaining care is to be withheld under certain circumstances. Typically a DNR order means that, should a sudden cardiac or respiratory arrest occur, there are to be no staff efforts to restore the heart beat or breathing of the patient. DNR orders may be written simply as the abbreviation "DNR" (especially if the hospital has a protocol that defines what this abbreviation means) or a DNR order may specifically describe the extent of life sustaining care to be rendered such as "if cardiac arrest occurs, provide oxygen by mouth but do not perform external chest compression."

Electrocardiogram (ECG or EKG)
a test which produces a graphic display of the electrical activity of the heart. These electrical patterns can be used to determine heart rhythm or damage to different chambers of the heart.

Electro-encephalogram (EEG)
a graphic display of the electrical activity of the brain. This display can be used to determine whether abnormal electrical activity exists. Abnormal activity is associated with certain disease states. May be used to help diagnose seizures or to assist in diagnosing brain death.

Electro-shock therapy (ECT)
the use of electrical shock to induce pronounced generalized irregularities in brain function. This effect is usually transient and may be used as a form of therapy in selected psychiatric disorders.

Embolism
an immediate obstruction to an artery or vein by a blood clot or other substance that has traveled through the blood stream from a distant site. Also see thrombus.

Endometriosis
a condition in which tissue similar to that of the inner lining (endometrium) of the uterus is present in an extrauterine place, such as on the outside of the uterus but inside the abdominal cavity. Pain may occur in association with menstrual cycles and at other times.

Endoscopy
see *oscopy*

Endotracheal tube usually a plastic, flexible and hollow tube, about twelve inches long (adult size), that is inserted into the windpipe and usually connected to a mechanical ventilator for assisted breathing.

Extubation the act of removing an endotracheal tube from the windpipe of the patient. The removal usually means that the patient no longer needs respiratory support or assistance from a mechanical ventilator.

Fellow in academic teaching centers, this individual is a physician who has graduated from medical school and also completed residency training but is now pursuing post-graduate education in a medical subspecialty such as cardiology.

Fibrillation refers to fibers. When used in association with heart rate disorders, it usually implies that the individual's heart muscle fibers are not contracting synchronously. The term fibrillation refers to a condition of irregular twitching or convulsing movement of heart muscles. The term can be applied to various areas of the heart such as atrial fibrillation or ventricular fibrillation.

Glomerulo- nephritis an inflammation of the kidney specifically affecting its small filtering units which are called glomeruli.

Heart attack an acute medical illness resulting from lack of blood supply to the heart muscle. Commonly characterized by severe chest pain, shortness of breath, and abnormalities in heart rate and rhythm.

Hemodialysis see *dialysis*

Hernia· the protrusion of a piece of tissue through an abnormal opening. Inguinal hernia means a protrusion of intestinal loops or tissue through the inguinal canal and into the scrotum sac. Hiatal hernia means protrusion of the upper part of the stomach through the esophageal canal of the diaphragm.

Hysterectomy surgical removal of the uterus. If the surgical approach involves incision through the abdomen or vagina, then the terms abdominal hysterectomy or vaginal hysterectomy are used respectively.

Ileostomy surgical procedure which creates an artificial opening in the abdominal wall to allow exit of the contents of the ilium (see also *colostomy*).

Intern a physician who has graduated from medical school but who is in his/her first year of "apprenticeship." In most areas, before a physician can be fully licensed to practice medicine, he/she must complete at least one year of internship training.

Intravenous inside the vein. Various solutions or medications are administered intravenously.

Intubate The act of inserting a breathing tube (endotracheal tube) into the trachea by passing it through the mouth or nose, down the throat, past the larynx and into the windpipe.

Isolation a type of quarantine procedure used to control infectious disease. Procedures may vary depending on how a disease is transmitted. If only wound secretions are isolated, then the term "wound isolation" may be used and relatively normal guest visitation otherwise is possible. Similarly, stool isolation may be employed. Respiratory isolation and strict isolation usually require more stringent quarantine on visiting guests (see *reverse isolation*).

Jaundice derived from the French *jaunisse* referring to yellow. Jaundiced skin color is usually the result of liver failure. The skin becomes yellow because the breakdown product of red blood cells, bilirubin, is not adequately removed from the body by the normal activity of the liver (see *bilirubin*).

Laminectomy refers to excision of a layer. A surgical procedure involving removal or aspiration of the vertebra disk, most commonly performed to help relieve back pain.

Laparotomy derived from the Greek "lapara," meaning flank. An operation involving cutting through the flank or abdominal wall. Exploratory laparotomy means an operation to evaluate the condition of abdominal organs.

Leukemia a word of Greek origin, meaning "white blood." A group of many diseases which cause an excessive, unregulated production of white blood cells. This disorder is a malignant disease and many forms (e.g., monocytic, lymphycytic, histiocytic) have different prognoses.

LPN licensed practical nurse. Licensed practical nurses have usually had two years of training. Licensed practical nurses are able to administer medications and to do many routine nurse functions without direct supervisions by a registered nurse.

Lumbar puncture (LP) a procedure whereby a sample of spinal fluid is obtained from the lower spine. A needle is inserted between the vertebral bodies until the needle enters a small canal containing cerebral spinal fluid. Usually, 1–3 cc's of fluid are removed and can be examined to diagnose central nervous disease.

Lupus erythematosis a disease of unknown etiology which involves a chronic inflammatory problem of many tissues. Common effects are inflammation of the kidneys, arthritis-like symptoms, and skin rash. Many other clinical abnormalities are also seen.

Magnetic resonance image (MRI) see *nuclear magnetic resonance*

Malignant derived from the Latin "malignans," meaning acting maliciously. A medical term used by pathologists to denote the cancerous condition of cells examined under the microscope. Malignant can also be used to refer to serious disorders such as malignant hypertension or malignant high blood pressure. All cancers are composed of malignant cells, but not all malignant medical conditions are due to cancerous conditions.

Mammoplasty a surgical operation resulting in tissue reconstruction of the breast. This procedure may be used to decrease or increase the size of the breast or to correct disfigurement caused by disease or injury.

Mastectomy derived from the Greek "mastos," meaning breast. Literally means removal of the breast. Radical, complete, or partial mastectomy refers to various surgical procedures used to remove all or part of the breast tissue.

Metastasis refers to the spread of cancer from its original site of development to distant places in the body. "Meta" means to change over and "statis" means to stand. Common sites of metastasis involve liver, lung, bone, and brain.

Myocardial infarction (MI) infarct refers to an area of tissue death caused from lack of blood supply, often due to a blocked or occluded blood vessel. When heart muscle is involved, the term myocardial infarction is used. It means the same thing as a heart attack. A myocardial infarction can involve only a small portion of heart muscle or can be very extensive causing failure of the heart muscle to adequately pump blood.

Necrosis death of tissue. Can refer to individual cells or to large areas of tissue. Often occurs after extensive injury or from infection or lack of proper blood supply to tissues.

Nephritis an inflammation of the kidneys. Many types of inflammatory kidney conditions exist (see *glomerulo-nephritis*).

NPO abbreviation meaning nothing is to be given to the patient by mouth. A common order usually written before major operations or used for individuals who are too severely ill to receive foods orally.

Nuclear magnetic resonance (NMR) a diagnostic method which provides detailed internal pictures of the body by recording the energy emitted from body tissues when the patient is placed in a strong magnetic field.

Oscopy a term used to name a procedure which usually means that the physician is directly looking at an internal part of the body. Examples include;
Laparoscopy - view of abdomen
Endoscopy - of stomach and duodenum
Esophagoscopy - of esophagus
Colonoscopy - of colon
Cystoscopy - of bladder
Bronchoscopy - of bronchi and lungs
Laryngoscopy - of larynx

Ostomy a door or opening. Commonly refers to canals or openings which are created by surgical procedures. For example, tracheostomy refers to the creation of an artificial airway between the neck and the trachea (see *colostomy* and *ileostomy*).

Palliative a treatment which provides relief but does not cure. Often used to describe treatments offered for selected types of cancers.

Peritoneal dialysis see *dialysis*

Phlebitis inflammation of the blood veins. Often occurs after a vein has been blocked by a blood clot (thrombus). Accordingly, the term thrombophlebitis is used.

Pneumo-encephalogram an x-ray procedure used to obtain information about the structure of the brain, especially cavities within the brain. In this procedure, air is injected into the spinal fluid by insertion of a needle into the low spinal area. The air is then allowed to transit up the spinal cord into various areas of the brain. X-rays then demonstrate the presence of air which outlines brain structures.

Pneumothorax an abnormal medical condition whereby air is present within the chest cage but outside of lung tissue.

This causes compression or collapse of the lung. Often occurs after traumatic injury to the lung but can occur spontaneously. Small amounts of air may not cause problems, but large amounts of air can cause respiratory distress.

PRN abbreviation often used in medical orders which means that a treatment, medicine, or procedure is to be used as the situation or circumstance requires. Pain medication orders are often written PRN so they may be given as needed.

Proctoscope derived from the Greek "proktos," meaning anus. A proctoscope is a tubular instrument which is inserted into the anus and is used to visualize the inside of the rectum.

Prognosis the prediction regarding the probable result, course, or outcome of a given illness. Example, the prognosis for survival five years from the onset of the illness is 80%. That is, 80% of patients will survive after five years of enduring the illness. Statements such as "the prognosis is poor" should be further clarified so as to provide more precise meaning and information.

Prostate a small gland in the male that encircles the neck of the bladder and the urethra. Disease which causes enlargement of the prostate can narrow or obstruct the urethra.

Protocol a preliminary outline or procedure. Used in medicine to refer to standard treatment procedures. For example, childhood leukemia may be treated using a specific protocol involving chemical and radiation therapy which is administered in specific doses and times. Protocols may involve standard, accepted medical practice or may represent very new treatments under investigation or research to determine effectiveness.

Pyelogram (Intravenous pyelogram or IVP) an x-ray picture of the kidneys and major draining systems (urethers). The x-ray picture is obtained by injecting into a vein a chemical which is concentrated by the kidneys and then visualized by x-rays.

Radiation electromagnetic energy in the form of waves, such as light waves, which are given off or emitted from some source. Radiation treatments are used to reduce the rapid growth of tumors or other diseases characterized by increased growth of cells. The high energy content of the radiation damages or kills rapidly growing cells.

Resident in hospitals with training programs for physicians, a resident is a physician who has graduated from medical school and is receiving training in a given field of medical practice. Residency training programs usually last from one to four years. The first year of residency training is often referred to as the internship year.

Respirator see *ventilator*

Respiratory therapy a form of therapy which attempts to improve lung function. The term is usually used to refer to a group of health professionals who are responsible for operation and maintenance of mechanical equipment in a hospital. They may also be responsible for obtaining an analysis of arterial or venous blood samples to determine if proper oxygenation is occurring.

Reverse isolation a form of isolation where the visitor is isolated from the patient. Usually used to protect patients who have easy susceptibility to common infectious diseases.

RN registered nurse. Usually an individual with four years of college training. The RN is responsible for coordinating and implementing the general nursing care of hospitalized patients and may supervise licensed practical nurses (LPNs), nurse aids, or other nurse assistants.

Sarcoma a tumor involving connective (e.g., bone, muscle, blood, ligament) muscle tissue. A muscle tumor associated or mixed with bone tumors may be termed an osteosarcoma.

Sepsis (Septicemia) both of these terms refer to the presence, in the blood, of bacteria or bacterial toxins. The presence of such usually requires intensive antibiotic treatment.

Septal defect septum means a dividing wall or partition and is a general term used in anatomical classification. Two common septums are the atrial septum, which separates the right and left atria, and the ventricular septum which separates the right and left pumping chambers of the heart. Any hole or abnormal communication in these septums is referred to as a septal defect. Septal defect is usually used in reference to heart abnormalities, although many other septums exist in the body, such as the nasal septum, and defects in these septums could also be referred to as septal defects.

Sexually transmitted disease (STD) an infection that is usually, but not invariably, transmitted by sexual intimacy. Common sexually transmitted diseases include:
Syphilis
Genital herpes infection
Venereal warts
AIDS
Chlamydia infection
Gonorrhea

Staphylococcus, streptococcus common bacteria which are present in normal individuals but which, under certain circumstances, can cause infections.

Stroke a sudden, severe attack such as an immediate onset of paralysis. Usually refers to a sudden occlusion or hemorrhage of an artery inside the brain. This causes discrete areas of brain tissue to be injured or killed. Transient or permanent paralysis or other abnormalities in neurologic function can result.

Supportive care only (SCO) usually a type of medical, limited-care order indicating that limitation is to be placed upon the extent to which otherwise aggressive and complete care would be given. Usually associated with a do not resuscitate order or other orders indicating limits to certain life sustaining treatments.

Thromboembolism   see *thrombus*

Thrombus   a blood clot that is inside a vein. When a venous blood clot breaks free and is carried to a distant site (usually causing injury or obstruction), the term thromboembolism is used.

Total parenteral nutrition (TPN)   a form of intravenous nutritional therapy whereby a mixture of amino acid, fats, and carbohydrates are administered. This form of nutrition requires careful attention to sterility and monitoring of the patient's clinical and laboratory condition.

Tracheostomy   an incision into the trachea through the skin and muscles of the neck usually for access to the airway, removal of a foreign body, or for the purpose of obtaining a biopsy.

Transurethral resection (TUR)   a surgical procedure which removes part of the prostate gland by surgically widening the urethra at its passage through the prostate gland (see prostate).

Tubes   when tube feeding is used, different types of tube feeding methods may be designated by abbreviations denoting the anatomical location of the tube. For example:

NG tube: a nasogastric tube going through the nose and into the stomach.

OG tube: a orogastic tube through the mouth into the stomach. Both NG and OG tubes can also be used to decompress or vent the stomach, thus preventing gaseous distention in an ill patient.

G tube: a gastrostomy tube that is surgically inserted directly through the skin and abdominal wall, on the left side, into the stomach.

NJ tube: a nasojejunal tube that passes through the nose, past the stomach and duodenum, and into the jejunal area of the intestine. Often used to prevent vomiting of feedings and regurgitation of stomach contents.

Ultrasound a diagnostic method which uses the reflection of sound waves to outline the anatomy of the body. For example, abdominal ultrasound may be used to outline the size of the kidneys.

Ureter the small fibro-muscular tube which transmits urine from a kidney to the bladder.

Urethra the canal which allows urine to exit from the bladder to the outside of the body.

Vectorcardiogram similar to an electrocardiogram except the electrical activity of the heart is graphically displayed in such a way as to provide more information about the direction and magnitude of muscle forces.

Ventilator a electrically powered machine, essentially an air compressor, that pushes air or oxygen enriched air into the lungs. Physicians oversee and manage their use but specifically trained respiratory therapists provide service, maintenance and hour-to-hour monitoring of ventilators in most hospital settings.

Ventricle a small cavity. May refer to one of several small cavities inside the brain which contains cerebral spinal fluid or may refer to one of the two major pumping chambers of the heart.